Nine Mile Bridge

Three Years in the Maine Woods

By Helen Hamlin

Nine Mile Bridge

Three Years in the Maine Woods

By Helen Hamlin

ISLANDPORT PRESS

YARMOUTH • FRENCHBORO • MAINE

Maine books from Islandport Press
www.islandportpress.com

The Cows Are Out!
by Trudy Chambers Price

A Moose and a Lobster Walk into a Bar
by John McDonald

Silas Crockett
by Mary Ellen Chase

Here for Generations: The Story of a Maine Bank and its City
by Dean Lawrence Lunt

In Maine
by John N. Cole

The Story of Mount Desert Island
by Samuel Eliot Morison

A History of Little Cranberry Island
by Hugh L. Dwelley

Hauling by Hand: The Life and Times of a Maine Island
by Dean Lawrence Lunt

Children's Books

When I'm With You
by Elizabeth Elder; illustrated by Leslie Mansmann

Please visit www.islandportpress.com for more information about all the great books available from Islandport Press.

Reading Groups
To find Reading Group questions related to *Nine Mile Bridge* or to find suggestions for further reading on the North Woods of Maine, please visit www.islandportpress.com/ninemile.

Islandport Press Inc.
P.O. Box 10
Yarmouth, Maine 04096
www.islandportpress.com

ISBN: 978-0-9671662-5-4
Library of Congress Control Number: 2004114785

First Islandport Press Edition, January 2005
Second Islandport Press Edition, March 2006
Third Islandport Press Edition, May 2010

Book design by Michelle A. Lunt / Islandport Press Inc.
Book jacket design by Karen F. Hoots / Hoots Design
Front and back cover photos courtesy of Helen Hamlin

To
Curly

Contents

Helen Hamlin

Helen Hamlin was born and raised in Maine, an Aroostook County gal through and through, with a love of the outdoors that permeated her very soul, but did not cast any shadows over an expansive view of the greater world or quench a thirst for adventure. She may have known how to hunt and survive in the unbroken, snowbound isolation of the North Maine woods, but she would also joyously travel the world from Russia to Australia and serve as a French translator for the U.S. State Department in Africa. She was a fisherwoman, a teacher and an accomplished painter who haunted the art museums of Europe.

Photo courtesy of Helen Hamlin

Helen Hamlin, 1940s.

"She led a very interesting

Helen Hamlin canoeing at Chase Carry, 1962.

life," said Catherine "Kate" Murphy, her youngest daughter. "She was, in many ways, a renaissance woman."

Helen Leidy (1917-2004) was raised in Fort Kent, a border town at the extreme northern edge of Maine with heavy French-Canadian influence, and she was surrounded by a large and closeknit extended family. Above all else, she loved the outdoors, loved the idea of adventure, and spent childhood summers at her grandfather's camps on Cross Lake, which is located on the Fish River chain of lakes. During those precious summers, she explored the nooks and crannies of the Fish River chain, taking long canoe trips to explore and fish for landlocked salmon and brook trout. She came by it all naturally; both her father and her grandfather were fish and game wardens.

Helen was also the oldest of six children—all bilingual—born to Mason (a veteran who is buried at Arlington National Cemetery) and Ella (Austin) Leidy. As the oldest, it fell to Helen

Photo courtesy of Helen Hamlin

Helen on Chamberlain Lake, 1980.

to help raise her younger siblings—making sure they had what they needed, and even snowshoeing them to school, if that is what it took.

She graduated from Fort Kent High School in 1935 and attended the old Madawaska Training School, a school that trained teachers, as she said, "to cope with the language problem in the St. John Valley." Many people in the region spoke French as their primary or even sole language. Hamlin was fluent in French.

During her days at the school, she listened intently as the principal told of his adventures hunting and fishing in the St. John River regions, and she was fascinated by his tales of the remote towns and lumber camps. Upon graduation in 1937, she requested a teaching position in a backwoods settlement, and her wish was granted. She took a job in the isolated lumber camp of Churchill Depot, located on Churchill Lake at the headwaters of the Allagash River. It was an undeniably lonely outpost—and rough around the edges.

"The settlement at Churchill was a lumberjack colony and was considered too wild and desolate for a woman teacher, but since I could speak French and had asked for a backwoods school, I became the first woman schoolteacher of Churchill," Hamlin said.

That surprised at least a few people, including the U.S. customs officer at Lac Frontiere, who offered the unheeded warning: "That is no place for a woman."

Her schoolhouse was a small log cabin, and she taught sixteen children, including some who spoke only English and some who spoke only French.

But Hamlin adjusted well, relishing the adventure even as life was tinged with hardship.

"I wouldn't go so far as to say that I could gladly spend the rest of my days at Churchill. I think very few people would say that—though I certainly never regretted going there. . . .

To this day I have not forgotten the many times I wished for a real bathtub with plenty of hot water and soap, instead of the inadequate white bowl in my cold room."

Needless to say, the young schoolteacher was popular in the male-dominated camp, and suffered from no lack of attention or wedding proposals when the lumberjacks were not in the woods.

Churchill Depot was remote, but its winter isolation was nothing compared to where Hamlin spent her next three years—places where she quickly learned the meaning of snowbound.

It was while teaching at Churchill that she met a well-known fish and game warden, Willis "Curly" E. Hamlin. Curly Hamlin, who was born in Brownville in 1908, had already spent fifteen years as a warden at Greenville, as well as additional time on the Canadian border. They married in September 1938, and that winter were stationed in a cabin on Umsaskis Lake. They spent the following two winters in a camp at Nine Mile Bridge. For large stretches of that time the couple was snowbound and utterly alone. They were miles from their nearest neighbors, and there were only a handful of people living within the thousands of square miles of wilderness they called home.

As the months dragged on that first year, Hamlin wrote, "With each snowstorm we felt less and less delight in its clean white beauty, because it reminded us of the long months to come and of the smallness of our little world at Umsaskis. Despite my love of the woods, I confess that sometimes I found the enforced solitude almost unbearable.

"The days were long, and many, many hours I just sat, watching the fire through the open drafts on the hearth, day-dreaming and not interested in much of anything."

Exacerbating their plight the first winter was poor planning—they began to run out of supplies. They began "baking" radio batteries each night in an effort to extend their life and get a few minutes of precious news each evening, but that eventually failed. Finally, when they essentially ran out of food and grew "so sick of cornmush and those nauseatingly pale beans that another meal would have been the final outrage"—they decided to brave winter conditions and snowshoe thirty-eight miles through the harsh and frigid wilderness to find food and, perhaps best of all, escape their isolation.

The following year at Nine Mile Bridge, they were better prepared, but no less isolated.

Through it all, Helen Hamlin hunted, fished, cooked, cleaned, showshoed, canoed, drove dogsleds and walked through unbroken wilderness.

By that summer, Helen was set to give birth to the couple's daughter, Susan Elizabeth Hamlin. In addition, Curly was ill, so the couple left the wilderness for civilization and settled for a short time on Norway Lake.

Helen chronicled her adventures in *Nine Mile Bridge: Three Years in the Maine Woods*, which was released by W.W. Norton and Company in 1945 and spent weeks on *The New York Times* best-seller list. The book—heralded as "Straight from the pine-scented forest of Maine"—catapulted her to some fame and notoriety within Maine as well as some outside literary circles.

Her success was enough that she used some of the proceeds from the book to help the couple buy the famed Parmachenee Club on Parmachenee Lake. They officially began operating the Club in 1946. Helen, given her experience, could work when she wanted as one of the fishing guides.

However, that same year, Helen and Curly divorced, and her local fame was such that when she filed for divorce, it merited a large photograph and story on page 1 of the *Lewiston Sun-Journal*.

Photo courtesy of Helen Hamlin

Helen Hamlin and her youngest daughter, Catherine.

Curly did not live long after the divorce, dying in Milo in August of 1948. He was just forty.

Although Helen's life in the wilderness had been over for some time and she was now a single mother, in some ways her adventures were just beginning. She ran the Parmachenee Club and, most importantly, she was about to fall in love again. This time it would last.

In 1947, she married Robert E. Lennon, a young man from Berlin, New Hampshire, a graduate student who also worked as a cruiser for a local timber company. The couple would eventually have three children together, Michael, Catherine and Christopher. Lennon's studies and career would also take Helen from Maine.

Lennon's research as he pursued a doctorate in ichthyology at the University of Michigan and his subsequent career would take the family out of New England to Michigan and to glorious trout streams in the Great Smoky Mountains and the Mississippi Valley in the upper Midwest. They eventually returned to Maine again to live when Robert's final assignment was heading up a salmon research project. They couple then built a retirement home near Lincoln in the 1970s.

During this time of moving around and raising children, Helen drew on her many talents to help earn money. She was an accomplished painter (some of her work hung in shows in Washington, D.C.) who specialized in portraits. While the children were in school, the famous and not-so-famous would come to her house to sit for commissioned portraits.

She would also continue her education to bring her teaching credentials current in French at the University of Wisconsin and the Sorbonne in Paris. She became a teacher again, and taught French at all levels from junior high school to college.

Before and after she retired from teaching, she continued traveling the world, including visits to Scandinavia, Russia, Egypt, Israel, Greece, Morocco, Australia, and China.

Helen also spent parts of six years working for the U.S. State Department as a translator in French-speaking equatorial Africa. She accompanied Robert, who was working with the World Health Organization and the United Nations in an effort to combat river blindness disease in West Africa.

Eventually, she slowed down and spent some of her time painting in Florida and California before retiring to Minnesota. Robert, her husband of more than five decades, passed away in 2004.

In addition to *Nine Mile Bridge*, Helen also wrote *Pines, Potatoes and People: A Story of Aroostook* (1948). And she enjoyed more fanciful writing later in life, penning several unpublished science fiction books. Helen died in Minnesota in 2004.

Photo courtesy of Helen Hamlin
Helen fishing in the Great Smoky Mountains National Forest, 1955.

Despite her travels and the time she spent living out-of-state, Maine was always a treasured part of her life. She loved her home state and she tried to pass that affection onto her children—taking them to many of the great rivers, lakes, and little-known wilderness spots that she cherished so much and that had so affected her life.

Said her daughter, Kate: "She made sure we knew that Maine was part of our legacy."

Dean Lawrence Lunt

Foreword

by Dean B. Bennett

Helen Hamlin has given us a rare and intimate view of a time when the northern wildlands and a way of life, both important to our natural and cultural heritage, were at the onset of dramatic change. In the heart of Maine's North Woods during the late 1930s and early 1940s, she lived on the shores of the legendary Allagash and St. John rivers—still known today as the two wildest rivers in the East. Her descriptions vividly illuminate images of a vast, remote, lonely, and heavily forested land of timber and wildlife on which a rugged, hardworking culture depended for its survival. While living in a logging settlement as a teacher, and later in a remote cabin as the wife of a game warden, Hamlin saw and experienced everyday moments of pleasure and excitement interspersed with disappointment and hardship. Her book records in human terms details of this life in our northern forest that would otherwise fade from our collective memory and be lost forever.

During her first spring, Hamlin flew over Churchill Depot at the head of the Allagash River where she had just spent the winter. The small settlement "was insignificant compared to the uninterrupted forest surrounding it—farther than the eye could see." Flying east to Portage, Maine, some fifty miles away, there was "nothing in between—no people, no habitation, no roads— nothing but what seemed like a thousand lakes and ponds." This picture of the North Woods more than a half century ago makes a unique contribution to our understanding of changes that have occurred since then.

Those changes were already under way during Hamlin's experience. It was a time when roads were beginning to open the woods, forewarning the end of the river drives and the region's desolate remoteness. Foresters and game wardens had begun using airplanes in their work, and sportsmen were discovering the ease of flying into remote streams and lakes for hunting, fishing, and trapping. Scientific forestry and an emerging view of the forest as a farm were directing the use of new methods and bigger equipment in timber harvesting. Trucks were not only beginning to carry logs out of the woods but were bringing supplies in as well, spelling the demise of the large farms in the woods that once supplied the logging operations.

Helen Hamlin glimpsed this changing way of life personally and poignantly at the end of her first spring at Churchill Depot, a time when the snowmelt began, river ice turned bluish, and trees grew dark and glistening wet. After "the fast-melting snow and small brooks swelled the river, breaking away the imprisoned ice in a grinding roar, the exuberant energies of the men were diverted to the drive," she tells us. But then, unexpectedly, the company closed its camp, and she left "with a real sense of loss" for what had become almost a "ghost settlement."

"The day may come when isolated lumber camps and river drives will be seen no more in Maine. . . . When conservation replaces the robber-baron tactics of landowners and 'big lumber men,' perhaps the great-great-grandchildren of this generation will once more know the forests of our grandfathers," Hamlin writes. And, indeed, the idea of conservation and its influence on the future preservation of the wild character of the two rivers had already begun, reflecting the beginning of our nation's changing views of wild land. Even before she left the region, there were people entering its woods and waters who saw values other than its long lumber and pulpwood.

Less than a decade and a half after this book was published in 1945, a team from the National Park Service passed by the abandoned boardinghouse and warden's cabin where Hamlin lived during her two years on the Allagash River. That group was investigating the Allagash River basin as a national recreational area. Others followed with a conservation bent, reflecting worries about the loss of the region's uniqueness in the East as a wilderness canoe experience. They included national and state figures who brought the preservation of the river to the attention of the Maine Legislature and the Congress of the United States. Their efforts culminated in 1966 with Maine's creation of the Allagash Wilderness Waterway—a strip of public land averaging 500 feet in width surrounding the vast headwater lakes and river of the Allagash watershed, some 250 miles of shoreline to be developed for its "maximum wilderness character" and buffered by controls over private land a mile beyond.

Helen Hamlin could never have imagined that twenty-five years after her book was published, U.S. Senator Edmund S. Muskie of Maine would stand as the featured speaker at an improvised lectern at the abandoned settlement of Churchill Depot, his backdrop the decaying boardinghouse where she had lived. Before him were dignitaries representing forest landowners, conservationists, and state and federal government. They had assembled for the dedication of the Allagash River and its headwaters as a state wilderness waterway, and as the first state-managed river in the newly created National Wild and Scenic Rivers System—both of which Senator Muskie had been instrumental in helping to bring about. The old dam that Helen had lived beside at the head of the river and that had washed out in the late 1950s had been replaced by one designed to control water for canoeists rather than for the transport of logs in the river drives.

Following Hamlin's second year in the North Woods, where she lived on the shore of Umsaskis Lake, some eleven miles downstream from Churchill Depot, she and her husband moved to a warden's camp on the St. John River at Nine Mile Bridge, named for the fact that it is nine miles above Seven Islands, an especially beautiful place on the St. John. This legendary river, too, is receiving increasing protection in both its headwaters and along its course, thanks to efforts by Maine's government, the Maine chapter of The Nature Conservancy, the forest industry, and many other contributors.

As Hamlin hoped more than a half century ago, the grand-children and great-grandchildren of her generation can still find in these great riverways a wilderness reminiscent of the way it was when she knew them. From the Allagash River's headwater lakes, canoeists can travel nearly a hundred miles northward to the village of Allagash, past a protected, nearly undeveloped shoreline, a rare occurrence in our nation. In this waterway, they can discover what Hamlin meant when she said, "There is an enchantment about the wilderness, especially to those who have lived in civilization. At first you are acutely aware of the 'wide open spaces feeling,' and then you grow accustomed to it and feel possessive."

Today, thousands of the grandchildren of Helen's generation have grown accustomed to and feel possessive about the Allagash and St. John rivers. They return by the thousands each year to enjoy the "dark quietness of the woods" and feel "the seasonal moods of the north woods lakes and rivers," which she wrote so knowingly about. They can visit stands of old trees along the shores of Eagle Lake that she saw as "somber giants passively brooding through the ages of time"; they can fish for togue and brook trout; they can encounter moose and deer along the shores, see eagles soaring and hear the wails of loons; and they can discover reminders of the wood's life she described— the site of Churchill Depot, the remains of the Tramway and the Eagle Lake–West Branch Railroad, and rusting Lombard loghaulers.

Near the end of her book, Helen Hamlin acknowledges, "the fascination of the wilderness isn't very easily explained." Yet, she has successfully done just that. I suggest that this book should be read by all who are contemplating a trip into the Allagash and St. John country, or who already have experienced it, or who merely have an interest in it and take satisfaction in knowing that these places that were part of her life still retain their wild beauty and fascinating history.

Dean B. Bennett
January 2005

Dean Bennett, born and raised in western Maine, is professor emeritus at the University of Maine at Farmington. He has devoted much of his professional life to teaching and writing in the fields of science and environmental education, natural history, and human relationships with nature. He has also been active in advocating for wilderness preservation and serves on the Allagash Wilderness Waterway Advisory Council. His books include: Allagash: Maine's Wild and Scenic River *(1994), a natural history, and* The Wilderness from Chamberlain Farm: A Story of Hope for the American Wild *(2001), a history of the Allagash wildlands. Bennett has canoed the Allagash since 1962 and he continues to write and illustrate books.*

"I was born in Fort Kent, Maine, one of the out-post towns of Aroostook County, and lived there until I was twenty. My summers were spent at my grandfather's camps on Cross Lake on the Fish River chain of lakes. By the time I was fifteen, I had explored most of the Fish River chain on long canoe trips. After high school, I went to Madawaska Training School, a normal school to train teachers to cope with the language problem in the St. John Valley. There I listened with eagerness when the principal told of hunting and fishing adventures in the St. John River territory, and thrilled to stories of life in the lumber camps; when graduation came I asked for and got the school at Churchill Lake, near the headwaters of the Allagash River. Then my adventures began. . . ."

Helen Hamlin

Chapter 1

Churchill Depot

My grandfather was a game warden, my uncle is a game warden and I married a game warden. I first met Curly when I taught school at Churchill Lake, the headwaters of the Allagash River in the wilderness area of northwestern Maine. The settlement at Churchill was a lumberjack colony and was considered too wild and desolate for a woman teacher, but since I could speak French and had asked for a backwoods school, I became the first woman schoolteacher of Churchill.

I arrived at Churchill in October, after a four-hundred-mile drive with my family. We had followed a roundabout scenic route, down the colorful back road from Fort Kent to Ashland, through the Mount Katahdin region, Baxter State Park, Ripogenus Dam and Moosehead Lake. From there we drove over the Great Northern Paper Company's private road to the boundary and into Canada.

At the St. Zacharie Hotel I had my first taste of wilderness hospitality. The rooms at the hotel were small, close and stuffy, and the plumbing was antique—of the chain-pulling era. The table in the dining room was set with a fancy glass service and with a bowl of store cookies for a centerpiece. The proprietress was a little, fat old lady with one tooth in her head. She was either very well pleased with herself or thought we were very funny, because she smiled broadly and continuously. We grinned back and ate the centerpiece—the store cookies—while waiting for the salt pork and fried eggs she had promised us.

The next morning we drove sixty miles through numerous small Canadian towns, and at Lac Frontiere we recrossed the boundary into Maine.

As we skirted the wilderness I had a preview of the surroundings I had chosen for what was to be, though I didn't know it at the time, the background of my first years of married life.

The American customs officer at Lac Frontiere was not encouraging. "You're the schoolteacher for Churchill?" he asked.

"That's right," I answered.

"Ever been there before?"

"No."

He offered an unheeded warning. "That is no place for a woman."

We showed our permit to go over the private road, and started the forty-three-mile drive to Churchill. The change in scenery was delightful. Where the Province of Quebec had been cleared and open, here was a forest of trees. The few cabins and camps along the way were picturesque and mostly deserted. The morning was lovely and cool, and the lifting mist revealed the brown road, the red, yellow, orange, wine and golden tints of fall. Held to a slow pace by the narrow, rocky road, we saw many deer and partridges. Once a black bear jumped out of a ditch and galloped ahead of the car. His flying paws threw gravel and stones back on the windshield before he disappeared abruptly off the road and crashed away through the underbrush.

Illustration by Helen Hamlin

An illustrated map of Maine.

Because I lived in Fort Kent—farthest northern outpost—I had heard many lumbermen, cruisers and guides speak of the vast, unpopulated timberlands on the headwaters of the Allagash and St. John rivers. To the majority of people, including those who live in the St. John Valley, this forest area is still the mysterious "backwoods."

A map of the state of Maine shows a large area along the Maine-Canadian boundary that has no highways or towns. It is dotted with lakes and ponds strung along the thin, twisty lines of the St. John and Allagash rivers and their tributaries. There are no highways. There are no towns. There are a few lumber camps but these are not shown on the map. If they were they would be too minute to be noticed, and too temporary for a surveyor to locate, even if he found them. Some maps show the private road that runs from the boundary into Churchill Lake, in the very heart of this forgotten country. The road penetrates but a short way into ten million acres of forest land, the largest unbroken wild timberland area in private ownership within the confines of any one state. The area is approximately 15,600 square miles of woods and lakes, and nothing else.

Edward La Croix, a Canadian lumber king, had logging operations on the St. John and Allagash rivers. He built the road in 1927 to carry supplies to his numerous and far-flung logging camps on the lakes and rivers. He built the steel bridge across the St. John River in 1931. The bridge had once been in St. Georges in the Province of Quebec, but was discarded because its width allowed only one car to cross it at a time. "King" La Croix transported the bridge piece by piece to the St. John River, and rebuilt it to replace the ferry that had been used there for so long. This was the bridge at Nine Mile.

There are a few log camps at the St. John River crossing and a small settlement at Clayton Lake. Side roads at Umsaskis lead to two lumber camps on the lake, and there is a fairly large settlement at Churchill Lake, at the end of the road.

I was deposited at the company boardinghouse, and my trunk was carried up to my room under the eaves.

"You're sure you won't go back with us?" Mother asked before leaving.

"I'm sure," I said.

They left me eagerly looking forward to eight months of winter. I had picked a ringside seat for a view to the inside of the country.

Suddenly a gong on the back porch rang to call the men to dinner, and I walked into the kitchen just as a motley crew filed through the door at the opposite end and silently seated themselves at the table. They were French Canadians—tall and short, young and old—unshaven, weather beaten, long haired and ragged. This was their appearance at dinnertime.

At suppertime, their appearance was quite different, though equally amazing. Every man jack was neatly shaven. Unruly hair was combed, brushed and anchored with water. Water still dripped from the long, plastered locks. Socks were straightened over boot tops and shirttails were tucked out of sight.

I had taken a seat at the foot of the table, but was later moved to the head. There are social distinctions in a lumber camp. Clerks, scalers, blacksmiths, mechanics, tractor drivers and truck drivers are given precedence over the common herd—the lumberjacks who sit at the foot of the table. The blacksmith and I, the schoolteacher, held down the bench at the head of the table.

Pea soup was passed around and I ladled a generous helping into the battered tin bowl I found upside down in front of me. Pots of tea and coffee followed the pea soup on the tour around the table, but the omission of a cup and saucer caused me to glance at the bent heads of my dinner companions. The man opposite me seemed to be an American.

Photo courtesy Maine Bureau of Parks and Land
Churchill Depot, possibly in the 1930s. The large building to the right is the boardinghouse where Helen Hamlin lived.

"What do we drink the coffee from?" I asked.

"Out of the bowl." He grinned and offered me his.

Joe Deblois, the man who had charge of the boardinghouse, interrupted by placing a cup and saucer at my elbow. I had committed a social error, and thereafter I ate pea soup in my plate and wiped it up with pieces of bread before the next course.

Food was good and plentiful. We had crispy roast beef for Sunday dinner, with little orange and yellow wheels of sliced carrots that were generously buttered and creamed. Golden potatoes were browned in meat gravy, and endless mounds of steaming, raised rolls kneaded and baked every day were appetizing enough for the most exacting gourmet.

The tables sagged under the weight of coffeepots, teapots, plates of apple pies, raisin pies, raspberry pies, sugar cookies, filled cookies and molasses cookies. The pea soup was the most delicious I have ever eaten. Whole peas were cooked in their own broth and were flavored with chopped green onion tops and salt pork. The rule was every man for himself—either grab what was passed down or grab what went back, with a real boardinghouse reach.

All table service was unbreakable enamelware, with a sturdy knife and fork beside each overturned plate and bowl. Spoons were in small canisters, clustered about with salt and pepper shakers, a bottle of vinegar, jars of pickles or relish, bowls of sugar, bottles of catsup and a homemade spicy sauce for which Joe Deblois would never give the secret recipe. In addition to all this there were the inevitable small jugs of molasses that every Old Timber Wolf pours into his plate at the end of a meal, to mop up with pieces of bread.

Under the watchful eye of Joe Deblois, we ate in silence, the unwritten but rigidly maintained custom of the lumber camp. We finished in silence, silently carried empty plate, bowl, knife, fork and spoon to the sideboard, and filed out. I continued silently up to my room, properly awed.

When there were just a few of us at the table, we talked. Everybody spoke French, but there were some who could speak English.

"You like him here, Mademoiselle?" I was once asked.

"Yes, I like it here. You speak English?"

"Ho yess, hi talk him leetle bit."

"Where you learn him?" I asked, catching on this time.

"Hi take her Great Norden hon top huff Pittston." Meaning, I learned it when I was working for the Great Northern at Pittston Farm.

"You like Pittston?"

"Ho no, she no talk *français*. Hi come home. You got feller?"

"No, I have no feller."

"Me, hi ham nize feller."

I switched to French for the others' benefit. "You are not the only one here. You are all handsome gentlemen."

A snicker went around the table.

"Me hi talk hinglise. Pass the macaroni *s'il vous plait*."

"Yes, pass the macaroni to the sheik."

Laughter.

Joe Deblois called for silence. "Eat, Big Nose. You have a wife at home."

Uproar.

I spent most of my first day unpacking in my small room. The walls were painted a battleship gray and the floors a shrieking orange, as were all the walls and floors in the boardinghouse. But the room was cheery with its bright-yellow curtains at the window, yellow spread on the wide bed, and colorful braided rug on the floor. There was a washstand with its usual white pitcher and bowl. Hooks were behind the door and on the wall for my clothes.

After scattering a few books, doodads and knickknacks around and hanging up clothes and pictures, I began to feel at home. I was much too excited with the strangeness and newness of my surroundings to feel lonely.

My first view of Churchill was not impressive. It wasn't what I expected. Churchill was a commonplace-looking settlement and not a romantic colony under the shadows of giant spruces. The lake was ghostly. The shores were lined with dri-ki, the bleached, dead stumps of drowned trees. Some were still upright, but most of them slanted every which way and were ready to disappear—the shameful traces of a dammed and flooded lake. The gates in the dam were partly open, and water rippled and cascaded over a rocky river bed. A little shed on the bridge held the dynamo that generated the electric current for all the buildings.

Most of the houses were identical, one-and-a-half-story company houses that had once been painted white. There were a few log cabins in the settlement, a few hen houses, woodsheds, outhouses, garden plots, and pigsties. The boardinghouse was a long, barrackslike building.

On the other side of the river was the company office, a more elaborate building that was occupied by a bachelor clerk who kept a Pomeranian dog. Lombard tractors, dual-wheeled trucks and small caterpillar tractors were housed and repaired in the long garage. A storehouse was filled with barrels of molasses or salt pork, cases of canned goods, flour, sugar, salt, dried fruits, cereals, axes, rope, peaveys, tobacco, kerosene and almost everything imaginable, all to be sold by the company to the people living at Churchill, or to be used in the lumber camps.

Today was Sunday, and the settlement was quiet. Doors were open to let in the late fall sunshine. Children were playing outside—the customary hopscotch and skipping rope. Boys toured the mud pond on their log rafts and fell in. Men stood in groups, talking. Some were dressed in store clothes—brown or blue suits—but most of them were dressed in the regular loose-fitting

Terence F. Harper Collection

The boardinghouse at Churchill Depot.

and well-worn breeches and woolen shirts. Women could be seen standing in the open doorways with arms crossed under aprons. Very few cars drove into Churchill.

A car stopped beneath my window and I leaned forward curiously, my nose pressed against the windowpane. Out of the back seat of the car tumbled a man—or boy—these French Canadians are so small in stature, I have difficulty in knowing which is which. His long hair was matted with blood and fell over an almost-closed black eye. One front tooth was missing. His white cotton shirt, a Sunday concession, was torn and bloody, and he was intoxicated beyond the point of belligerence. He had been well manhandled, when in the course of an argument he had threateningly brandished a small automatic.

There was much arm wagging—the punctuation to French conversation—before he was hustled into one of the houses to sleep it off. Someone looked up and caught me taking in the scene, and I drew back hurriedly, wondering if this colony was as tough as rumor claimed it to be. I didn't know it then, but this same follower of Bacchus was to be one of my bunk companions on a memorable night spent on McNally Pond, halfway to nowhere.

Such incidents were rare at Churchill and bore out the old Maine adage that I learned is still true: Never believe anything you hear, and only half of what you see. I did see a few drunken lumberjacks during my stay there, but they were the exception rather than the rule.

Liquor was hard to obtain, and was strictly forbidden in the camps. The lumberjack does not drink while in the woods for the simple reason that he can't get it. When spring comes and he gets out, he celebrates. Even then he is not so pugnacious. Like other people, there are the good and the bad, and the outstanding revelers have produced the impression that the lumberjack is a holy terror. The few drunken lumberjacks I have seen on their yearly benders were harmlessly merry or befogged with sleep.

I grew to like Churchill and all its drabness. The American customs officer at Lac Frontiere had been mistaken. There were several women at Churchill, mothers of large families and many girls who were no older than myself. There were a few English-speaking families scattered along the La Croix road and a definite majority of men—lumberjacks from a dozen camps around Churchill, likable, good-hearted and good-natured children of the forests.

On weekdays Churchill was a droning beehive. The storehouse was opened to the few customers. Sleds were loaded with supplies for a camp. The sawmill was in full buzzing swing, fragrant with freshly sawed pine and spruce. The noisy blacksmith shop was rosy with the glowing light from the forge. Hammers pounded and clanged all day as broken machinery was repaired or new logging chains and sleds were made.

Garage doors were open and the building reverberated with the muffled roar of a Lombard. The boardwalk to the office resounded to the heavy boots of lumberjacks going to and from the office. Tractors came down from the tote roads that branched out from Churchill. The muted hum of other tractors on hauling roads could be heard. Heavy trucks rumbled over the wooden bridge. The foaming water below the dam was never silent. The dynamo added its "watch-movement" throbbing.

Chapter 2

Everybody Swing!

I had been at Churchill three weeks when I was invited to attend a dance—a wedding reception that was to be held at Clayton Lake. Telesphore la Tour was a handsome fellow from one of the back camps. I didn't like his name. He was persistent, and as a further inducement to accept his invitation he suggested I would make him a good wife. My French could be polished a bit and he would buy me a new cookstove—a cream-colored one or a black and white one, I could have my choice, and if I were really fussy I could have one with a little window in the oven door so I could peek in and see how the bread was rising. Of course I had to refuse, not being quite ready to spend my time in the kitchen, for all his pretty brown eyes and black hair. However, I did go to the dance and had a wonderful time.

The week before the great event was busy and hectic. The sole topic of conversation was the dance. What are you going to wear and whom are you going with? The men brought in their Sunday suits to have them pressed, and the barbershop was open until late at night. The spirit was contagious. I spent hours in my room: Shall it be the green Paisley print or the pink skirt

and sweater? I settled for the green silk. Sweater and skirt
would be too informal for such an occasion.

When the great day came, I cautiously fished out my cosmetics from behind the washbowl and applied a bit of "drugstore face"—a caution I was to learn was needless, for it turned
out that I was ghostlike in comparison with even the most mod-
est demoiselle at the party.

We started for Clayton piled two deep in the cars. Telesphore
was quite enthusiastic about the arrangement and yelled to the
men at the boardinghouse to come out and witness the fact that
he was hugging the schoolteacher. Because Telesphore was merely
one of the lumberjacks, he didn't own a Sunday suit but was
dressed in his dark breeches and a brand new bright green checkered shirt. He didn't smell of shaving cream and tobacco as most
men do. He smelled of spruce on a windy day.

The dance at Clayton was held in the kitchen of the boardinghouse, a counterpart of the Churchill Lake boardinghouse.
The bride and groom had been married that morning, and the
dance was a reception and going-away party before the young
couple left on their short honeymoon.

Everyone was there from miles around. Churchill was repre-
sented by whole families: twelve Blanchettes, four Jeans, ten
Brocheaux, seven Veillieux and eight Paquets. There were two
hundred men from the back camps—mechanics, truck drivers,
scalers, clerks, cruisers, woods bosses, lumberjacks—and the few
and very popular girls in the settlement. There were English-
speaking fire wardens and game wardens from Umsaskis, Nine
Mile and Clayton, as well as the "walking boss" and the postmistress. Relatives of the bridal couple came from Lac Frontiere
accompanied by a sprinkling of belles and beaus. The belles

were generously dusted with powder, and the beaus were slickly plastered with brilliantine.

The kitchen and small living room were crowded with people in all styles of dress: the mail-order catalogue's latest fashions, and some not so late. There were two evening gowns amidst the black, red, green, blue and purple checkered shirts, patched and unpatched breeches and uniforms. Dorothy and Jack Butler made an impressive entrance, she in a flowing evening gown and he in a swallow-tailed coat with correct pants and dancing pumps. Hallie Dow in a pair of borrowed slippery Indian moccasins and a leather bow necktie. Gorgeous handkerchiefs blossomed forth from the breast pockets of Sunday suits, and the "more deadly of the species" were bedecked with necklaces, earrings, bracelets and flashy pins. The bride wore a brilliant cerise taffeta evening gown, and the groom, a blue-serge suit. They certainly were a handsome pair.

The air was so blue with cigarette smoke I could hardly see across the crowded room. Tables and benches were pushed against the wall and were weighted down with assorted humanity. The benches near the door were filled to overflowing with the pushing, struggling, impetuous and excessive stag line.

The mingled odors of sweat, stables, damp clothing, Fleur d'Amour talcum powder, greasy cosmetics and unwashed feet were overpowering, and a constant, confusing babble of English and French rose and fell like the tides.

Telesphore and I were swallowed by the mob that rushed to the center of the room when the dance caller announced a Lady of the Lake. To the tunes of old French reels, played by one violin, two harmonicas and the accompanying stamping of feet by the seated audience, we pranced and pounded the Boston Fancy, Lady of the Lake, Soldier's Joy, Sashey Up and Sashey Down,

Four Hands Around and Dive and Six. In the dimly lit room various encounters were made with the supporting posts in the middle of the floor, and as the music quickened, the circles of Sashey Up and Sashey Down swelled and intermingled.

The dances were called partly in English and partly in French; a Lady of the Lake sounded something like this: "*Balance* the side! *Balance* the center! *Promenade* the center! Back and *les bonnes femmes changeons*." And usually ended with what sounded like "*Les bonnes femmes sont chaudes!*" and "Ev-er-y-bod-y SWING!"

It was wonderful. Imagine my sensation as I was vigorously whirled in a Boston Fancy! My feet never touched the cornmeal powdered floor. I was tightly clutched to a violet-checkered shirt, and the skin peeled off the side of my face from the contact with day-old whiskers!

Then the orchestra struck up the "Isle of Capri"—we could always get back to earth on a waltz, then coming into fashion. We glided over the floor, calmly dodging caulked boots.

After each magnificent, breathtaking, spinning square dance, there was a lull for reinforcing refreshments. Misty and acrid home-brew and straight gin were passed around, and if anyone wanted an unheard of "chaser," why—have another gin! Cake, candy and cookies followed. A surprisingly small number of the lumberjacks were under the influence of "excessive refreshment," though when the best man started to deliver a political speech, he was unable to get beyond the words "*Mesdames et Messieurs*" when he was picked up and brushed off. During one of these brushing-off periods, he announced to the audience in general that he had a case of real Canadian ale in his truck, which intelligence resulted in a sudden falling off of the stag line—Telesphore included.

"You dance wit me, Mademoiselle?"

"*Oui.*" I was whirled away.

"You. Big girls." He beamed. He was four feet, two inches tall.

"So they tell me," I muttered.

"Wot dat?"

"I say it's the Aroostook potatoes. If you don't grow one way, you grow the other."

"Make good wifes." He was bursting with good intentions and I listened to the third proposal of the evening.

"Hall right, Halphonse, he's my turn now." I floated away with a red shirt and patched pants. Someone passed me a glass of home-brew with two dead flies floating around in it. The dance caller came to the rescue.

"Choose your partners! Four Hands Around!"

I headed for the door in search of fresh air and Telesphore. The early-fall night air was sharp and when my eyes had accustomed themselves to the darkness, I noticed a curious sight in the direction of the parked cars. The best man was doing a marionette dance outside his truck. I leaned over the railing to get a better look and discovered that a brawny arm was reaching out of the window of the cab, clutching the best man by his collar and holding him a foot off the ground. I caught a scrap of conversation.

"By damn me!" It was Telesphore displaying his English. "Dis man she's wiggle. You suppose we give her one bottle?"

Four other voices protested in French.

The bride and groom had disappeared long ago, and it was two o'clock in the morning before the grand rush to the bedroom to untangle wraps, scarves and sleeping babies.

Chapter 3

Mademoiselle la Maitresse

Monday morning I was slightly shaken but still able to limp around. There isn't anything quite as exciting or strenuous as a good old-fashioned "hawg-rassel." It takes a first-class athlete to stand up under the strain.

I missed the fall hunters when they left. I had enjoyed sitting in the living room and listening to them talk with their sharp New York and Boston accents. Very few hunters get up this far, and those who do come do so year after year. Since there are no camps for rent in the whole country, many of them stay at the boardinghouse. During the evenings they played cards in the kitchen, and I vividly remember the New Yorker who could play a harmonica and obligingly entertained us with any selection we asked for. Though the hunting season is open until the end of November, they had to leave earlier because steady storms were piling the snow three and four feet deep in the woods and closed the road through Canada. Churchill went into hibernation, and teaching school kept me busy.

Anna, Margaret and I spent the long winter evenings listening to the radio—we were devoted to the "Hit Parade"—playing cards or walking in the cold winter moonlight. Anna was the good-looking daughter of the people who had charge of the boardinghouse, and she spoke English as well as she spoke French. This was her first winter at Churchill, and like everyone who has finished school, we wistfully recalled the high-school dances we had attended.

Margaret was the red-haired and good-natured hired girl who took a lot of kidding about her carrot top. She spoke no English at all, but a strong, guttural, Quebec French that was difficult to understand. She taught me French Canadian ballads that amuse my husband when he hears them. His favorite, "Wee Willie Wink Paw" as he calls it, is really "Marie Madelain." This is the chorus.

Terence F. Harper Collection

Churchill Depot in winter.

Marie Madelain
Son petit jupon de laine,
(Her little woolen petticoat)
Sa petite jupe tricoté,
(Her little knitted skirt)
Son petit jupon piqué.
(Her little quilted petticoat)

In the Madawaska dialect it is quite different. This is what it sounds like. Roll the *r*'s and hiss the *s*'s. The *n* in the word *son* is very soft, such as the English word *song*, spoken quickly.

Ma-r-ree Ma-dee-len
Son seat joo-pon de len
Sa seat joop karrotée
Son seat joo-pon P-K

There is another one that doesn't make much sense to me. This is the first verse and the chorus.

C'était une jeunesse fille-a
(There was a young girl)
Qui n'avais pas quinze ans.
(Who was fifteen years old)
Elle s'en est dormi-a
(She went to sleep)
Au pied d'un rosier blanc.
(At the foot of a rose bush)

Son voile par ici, son voile par là
(Her veil this way, her veil that way)

Son voile qui volant, qui volant,
(Her veil that flutters, that flutters)
Son voile qui volant au vent.
(Her veil that flutters in the wind)

The ballads are much like western cowboy songs with a repeated chorus after each couplet or stanza. They describe the beauties of a belle, or tell of the hunting trip the king's son took. My favorite is the old paddling song of the French Canadian *voyageur*, "En Roulent Ma Boula" (Roll On My Little Boat).

Derrière chez nous il y a un étang,
(Behind the house there is a pond)
En roulent ma boula.
Derrière chez nous il y a un étang,
En roulent ma boula.
Trois beaux canards s'en va baigna,
(Three pretty ducks were swimming)
Roule, roulent, ma boula roulent,
En roulent ma boula roulent, en roulent ma boula.

Le fils du roi s'en va chassant,
(The king's son went hunting)
En roulent ma boula.
Le fils du roi s'en va chassant,
En roulent ma boula.
Visa le noir, tua le blanc,
(Aimed at the black, killed the white)
Roule, roulent, ma boula roulent,
En roulent ma boula roulent, en roulent ma boula.

22

We amused ourselves by trying almost every recipe we found in old magazines or newspapers, and if the results weren't what we expected, we had to eat the stuff anyway.

Mrs. Deblois kept her cookies in a jar on the sideboard, and I never went by without reaching in for a cartwheel cookie or a jelly-filled one. She would laughingly declare that a big mouse was in the cookie jar.

"May I have two?" I asked.

"*Oui*, Mademoiselle, have three or four, and have a glass of top milk, nice and cold and right off the ice."

I liked Mrs. Deblois. She called me "Mademoiselle la Maitresse." How nice that sounds!

Anna had a candy commissary in the kitchen where she sold chocolates and chewing gum, and the shelves and small counter were a great attraction. We were soon acquainted with some of the younger men who were set to work wiping the supper dishes, or we teased one of the scalers to cook us a spaghetti feed, and tormented the bashful blacksmith, whom Anna later married. Two boys, cookees, who peeled potatoes and did other odd jobs around the kitchen also had their share of kidding. They both had had permanent waves that fall, and during the winter they were loath to cut the crinkly locks that hung down over their ears like twin waterfalls.

Since I was able to speak French, I could join in the fun, but I was as puzzled by some of their idioms as they were at my attempts to express myself. They spoke a different French from mine. Theirs was slurring, and half the words were lost in throat rumbling—a Quebec French. The French I had picked up was by no means perfect. It was nasal and half English—a Madawaska French. If I wished to say "I do not understand," I would say *Je n'y comprendre pas*. They would have used the idiom

Cela me passe (It passes my understanding). The most familiar idiom I ever heard them use was *Il n'y a pas de quoi* (Don't mention it).

A great many lonely evenings were spent in my room, listening to the radio far into the night when the dance bands would be playing. Some of the songs that winter were "Remember Me," "You're a Sweetheart," "I Double Dare You," and "My Cabin of Dreams." And as I listened I would hear the wind whipping across the wide, white lake, howling like demons through the dri-ki, and mournfully whistling around the corners of the building. The powerful roar of a Lombard would break through the bleak desolation of those dreadfully cold, crackling nights as it rumbled down from the back camps and swept its searchlight over the darkened houses.

Chapter 4

French Canadians

I wouldn't go so far as to say that I could gladly spend the rest of my days at Churchill. I think very few people would say that—though I certainly never regretted going there. There was enough to keep me busy and enough novelty to keep me interested. Close association with this lost colony did scrape some of the glamour from it, but not all by any means. The people became real people and life while at times becoming humdrum nevertheless had its variations.

To this day I have not forgotten the many times I wished for a real bathtub with plenty of hot water and soap, instead of the inadequate white bowl in my cold room. Luckily, the only flush toilet in the settlement was in the boardinghouse. It was restricted to the family, myself, and the scalers and blacksmith. Sometimes the chain worked, but when it didn't there was a barrel of water handy and a ten-quart pail.

Although most of the families at Churchill were French Canadians and had lived in the woods all of their lives, they had one very human trait: family feudin'. Whether because of the isolation or despite it, feudin' was an indoor sport. Everyone had his resentments, and as I look back I think that I myself at first resented the "French school." Many of the children living at Churchill didn't come to the state school but attended a small French school, chiefly to learn their catechism, as decreed by their church, and simple addition and subtraction.

A youngster waited at the boardinghouse one afternoon with a message for me. "Mama say you come see her," he said.

I followed him to one of the small houses and was ushered into an immaculate kitchen.

"Sit down, Mademoiselle, and take your jacket off," his mother greeted me.

It was the first time I had been in one of these houses, and I looked around curiously. The rough board floor had been scrubbed and bleached with a brush and lye, and the kitchen stove, the heart of the home, was polished and gleaming. Six small, wide-eyed children sat quietly while we talked. I was surprised at her ability to speak English, and I remarked upon the fact, before coming to the point of the visit.

"I've read everything I have here and I wondered if you have any magazines I could borrow."

I replied that that was one of the things I had overlooked when coming up here. I was sorry I hadn't brought more books. "What do you usually read?" I asked.

"This." She brought out a battered copy of *True Story*!

Before I left I ventured to ask why her children didn't attend the state school. She was quite frank. "It isn't because we do not think the state school is good, Mademoiselle, but the children are so young to start to learn English. When they are twelve or fourteen, yes, but now we would not like to have them forget French, or their religion."

I knew that it was useless to argue. I had heard this argument before and knew how strongly they felt about the matter, so I dropped the subject. "Madam," I said, "what a beautiful stove!" I rubbed my hand over the flower-patterned porcelain tiles. "It is new?"

"No, it was my grandmother's. See." She pointed to the fine brown lines in the porcelain.

"But how do you keep it so glossy?"

"No water, Mademoiselle, just an oiled cloth," she stated proudly. "My grandmother told me that when she gave it to me."

These people lived a simple life. The families were large and closely knit, and everyone worked, from the youngest girl who washed dishes to the oldest boy who at fourteen or sixteen worked in the woods with his father. The women sewed, crocheted and knitted beautifully. The men worked as mechanics, jobbers or truck drivers for the lumber company, from whom most of them rented their houses.

The highlights in their social life were the dances, and though I attended those they had that winter, there was never anything to compare with the Clayton dance, which is still vividly remembered by those who were lucky enough to be there.

They bought their food from the company storehouse which was open three days a week. Some families owned cows, chickens and pigs, and they had fresh milk, eggs and butter. Beef was driven in on the hoof in the late fall, kept in the stables and slaughtered as it was needed. Clothing, household furnishings and little luxuries were ordered from mail-order catalogues, usually Sears-Roebuck—the "Woodsman's Bible."

Mail came to Clayton every day, and every other day the mailman drove to Churchill. When his battered coupé stopped in front of the boardinghouse, doors opened and the population congregated like chickens around a handful of corn.

"Monsieur Caron, have you a package for me?"

"There is something in the bag. It is big so I think it must be your package." Monsieur Caron handed the bag to the eager youngster, who clutched it tightly and ran for home. The mailbag was gently emptied on the kitchen table and the contents examined. There were new shoes for Gemma, new stockings for Camille, a new oilcloth for the table, new sheeting and a bundle of those odds and ends of cloth to make patchwork quilts that mail-order houses pack.

I had been at Churchill for some time and I still wondered where the men lived—those who came through the mystery door at the opposite end of the kitchen. I knew the blacksmith and scalers had rooms on the same side of the building as myself. I had heard the term "bar-r-room" and it puzzled me. At first I thought they meant a saloon, but since I didn't see any signs of liquor around, I asked Anna about it.

"That is the place where the men stay," she told me.

I was still puzzled.

"If you want to see it," she suggested, "I can show it to you on a Saturday afternoon when they are all at work."

She was as good as her word, and I felt like one of Bluebeard's wives when I walked through the door into the "bar-r-room." It was a large empty room with benches lining the walls, a sink and a sideboard in one corner, with a cracked and peeling mirror over it. The only breaks in the monotony of gray were the one or two religious pictures hanging on the walls and the gaily decorative red, green and white of double-knitted socks that were drying on a rack over the stove. The room was warm but cheerless.

The upstairs was divided into two bunkrooms. The room with the gabled window was reserved for the mechanics and truck drivers, and besides a row of board bunks there were two mattresses and a spring that were the personal property of some of the mechanics. The regular woods spreads—often called horse blankets—were used as blankets.

The other bunkroom was windowless and dark. Both walls were lined with an unbroken line of rough board bunks which were covered with woods spreads for the lumberjacks. A boarded-off corner of the room was used as a barbershop. It had a real barber chair, a mirror and a shelf full of implements of the trade. A truck driver did the barbering. The smell of unwashed bodies and stale air was strong. Anna remarked, a bit wistfully I thought, "You'd never know we had just cleaned this place."

"Is it really lousy?" I asked.

"Better not touch anything," she said.

The men brought the lice with them. Very few, if any, lumber camps are free from *Pediculus humanus*, *Pediculus capitis* and *Cimex lectularius*—in plain English, lice, cooties and bedbugs. The old story of a woods blanket walking across the floor to trip you may have some foundation of truth, but I never could believe the one about the lumberjack with the long hair who was dragged to the brook for a badly needed spring bath.

I noticed several cans of talcum powder on the little shelves over the bunks—Sweet Pea and Purple Passion. "Do they use that?" I was incredulous.

Anna laughed. "They think it keeps the lice away."

Most of the lumberjacks at Churchill were French Canadians from the new range roads in the Province of Quebec, and they were especially lenient in matters of personal cleanliness. To some of these backwoods range-road families, soap is a luxury.

These people are short in stature, nervous and thin, with sharp features, straight black hair and soft brown eyes that are probably an inheritance from Indian ancestors.

Nine Mile Bridge

Most of the French Canadians on our side of the boundary had papers giving them a legal right to be there. There were a few who had no papers. At certain intervals the Border Patrol would make excursions into Churchill to visit the lumber camps, but usually everyone in the country would know of their impending visit hours before they arrived. One very early mid-winter morning, however, the back camps were taken by surprise. Ten Border Patrolmen had come to Lac Frontiere by train and into Churchill and the back camps without anyone seeing them. The few outlaws in the camps immediately took to the woods, some of them only partly dressed. That morning at breakfast at the boardinghouse, the Border Patrol appeared with one victim. He hadn't been able to get very far on that cold winter morning, in just his long underwear.

For weeks afterward Churchill wondered how the raid had been pulled off, but it had its effect. Several of the uncaught culprits hurriedly came into Churchill, collected their wages and went back home. One cookee never came back to the lumber camp for his belongings, but started straight across country for the Canadian border, fifty miles away. How he ever made it through the deep winter snow, I never could imagine, but he did. We heard about it from his friends.

Not all the men who worked in the back camps were French Canadians. Some came from Aroostook County. Those who didn't speak French didn't stay long. A few were the true woodsmen from the little Allagash settlement at the mouth of the Allagash River. These woodsmen are in a class by themselves. They are intelligent, fine featured, tall, dark and always poised. I would recognize an Allagash man if I saw only the back of his head. Long years in the forest and on the river have given him an air of confidence that is unmistakable.

I met many of the men on my snowshoe hikes around the tote and hauling roads. Foolish of me, you say, to wander in the woods, watching the men at their work, sitting on the landings or lunching in the lumber camps. But I've rubbed elbows with lumberjacks ever since I can remember, and I've learned that the "wolves" do not live in the woods.

When I rounded a bend in the tote road, a scaler shouted: "It's the teacher! Hi, Mademoiselle, you want my job? I give you my caulk boots, and me, I teach school."

"Not today," I laughed. "This is Saturday."

"He's easy, jus' do dis." He ran his spoked wheel along the log, counted the red spoke as it came up, measured the center diameter with a caliper and referred to the Blodgett rule on the handle to determine the number of board feet in the log. He jotted it down in his little notebook.

Lumbering fascinates me. I was quite familiar with pulp cutting, but at Churchill they were cutting long lumber, which is an entirely different process. Lumbering itself is so complicated and carried on so differently in each section that with each new generation the operation is changed. The whitewater man—the "river hog"—the lumberjack who rode virgin timbers down undammed waterways is almost gone. There is very little of the first stand of enormous timber left, and damming the headwaters to control the supply of water subdues the power of a spring freshet.

Chapter 5

Lumbering

I t is perhaps unfortunate that the word "lumbering" suggests a colorful calendar picture of a "river hog" riding whitewater, rough and tumble scraps in caulked boots, rollicking shanty songs and Paul Bunyan's Herculean adventures, for lumbering is a more complicated operation than these romantic pictures would suggest. And it is a phase of American life that will one day disappear, leaving behind little understanding about old-time methods of lumbering, and the lumberjack.

The actual start of operations is cruising—a reconnaissance by men who know timber from experience and not necessarily from book learning. There are some college-educated cruisers who have been successful chiefly because they liked a wilderness life, but as a rule, cruisers are men who have lived close to the woods all of their lives, and have always known the ways of the forest and its inhabitants.

They know if a spruce is sound by the amount of pitch ooz-ing from it, and that the conks—or bunches—on a pine tree betray a rotten core. They know by tapping a tree with an ax whether it is fit for lumber purposes. Cruisers are sent by a lumber company to survey the tract of timberland to be cut, to estimate the approximate number of thousand board feet in the standing timber, or the cords of pulpwood.

Some cruising is done by finer processes. As nearly as possible the cruisers estimate the timber, measuring every tree with a caliper and guessing at the height. One method of determining the height of a tree is to cut a stick the length of the arm from elbow to hand. Hold the stick upright, grasping it at the bottom, and with the arm held straight out, walk backward until just the top of the tree is seen over the top of the stick. The distance from that spot to the butt of the tree is its height.

Success of the lumbering operation is partly due to the cruiser. He is a lone wolf and stands apart from the lumberjack. He is accustomed to traveling alone, and even in a crowd he will be noticed. His experience in lumbering ranges from cookee to lumberjack, scaler, or "woods boss." One of the most outstanding cruisers I knew was a French Canadian boy who started with no education whatever, but was not satisfied to be a run-of-the-woods lumberjack. He worked at everything he could find, and whenever he found himself working in a city he would attend night school, and so learned to read, write and speak English as well as French. At twenty-eight he was well known and in great demand by lumber companies.

The contract for the lumber to be cut may be divided among "jobbers"—lumbermen who proceed independently to fulfill the contract at their own personal loss or gain. Or the lumber company may hire a woods boss to fulfill the contract at stipulated wages, or a jobber may hire a woods boss to supervise the cutting. In large depot camps where many jobbers or woods bosses are employed, a "walking boss"—or superintendent—is hired by the company to see that everything is running on schedule. The walking boss also has charge of supplies, trucks, tractors, sleds and other equipment.

One of the boisterous phases of operating a lumber camp is the hiring of lumberjacks. Large companies hire them by the thousand through an employment agency, but the majority of small jobbers hire them by word of mouth in their own small community. One of the difficult parts of this process is to get the men to camp in a comparatively sober state. Once the first crew is there, and the fiery effects of "likker" have sputtered and died, the lumber camp is ready to take shape.

Tote roads are swamped—a simple process of clearing out trees, underbrush and other obstructions and taking the easiest way around big rocks, enormous tree trunks, ditches and sharp inclines, making a twisting and winding trail. Where the road runs along the ridge, the swamping is easy, but in marshlands, corduroy roads are built. Trees are felled, limbed and cut the desired width of the road, and a bridge is laid on the boggy land. The logs lie across the road and make a ridgy surface that is known as corduroy. The tote road is used solely for the transportation of men, materials and supplies to the camp site, and only during the winter, when the ground is frozen and the road is leveled with snow, can anything heavier than a horse go over it. The tote road is not built for posterity but is used only as long as the lumber camp is in operation.

There is a maze of bewildering tote roads in forest land that has once been cut over. Half of them are completely hidden by new, half-grown trees, but many are still used by woodsmen who wish to travel on foot across country or up and down the rivers. Tote roads along the Allagash and St. John rivers are still used, and the old tote road, the California Trail as it is called, from Ashland across to the boundary, is still used. Old tote

Pulpwood piled high on a frozen Heron Lake, which is part of Churchill Lake. The wood was piled high on the ice during the winter so that when the ice melted it would fill the lake and could then be driven via rivers during the spring.

roads are good hunting trails for the inexperienced hunter as long as when the time comes for him to start for home he can still remember which branch of the road he followed.

Logs for the camp are cut and peeled right on the camp site. The better camps are built in the spring when the sap is running and the bark peels off easily, but most camps are built of unpeeled logs. The camp grows as the logs are notched and laid one over the other, and the roof is the last thing added. Windows and doors are cut into the camp wall, and the sawed log ends are held in place by little wooden pegs that are driven into the logs below them. The finished camp consists of two separate rooms that are joined by a dingle—an open shed. In some camps the floors are small, peeled poles instead of rough boards, and some floors are just bare earth.

A bare earth floor in a camp always reminds me of one of those fantastic horror stories I've heard the lumberjacks tell. One time a scaler murdered another scaler and the cook witnessed the act. The murderer threatened to kill the cook too if the cook didn't help him dispose of the body and keep his mouth shut about it. The cook was too frightened to do anything else, and they buried the body in the dirt floor under the table in the cook camp. Years later, while lying on his deathbed, the cook confessed the deed, and when the skeleton was dug up, they found the bones mixed with a lot of the corncobs that the men always throw under the table.

On one side of the lumber camp is the kitchen and dining room combined. It is large and roomy and has rough board tables, benches, sideboards and shelves for supplies. Often there is a boarded-off corner where the cook and cookees have their bunks and belongings. The stove is a large wood-burning range. The plumbing is open, and the cookees haul water from a spring or brook. Sewage is dumped out the back door. Beating a gong—sometimes a dishpan and sometimes a wagon wheel rim—calls the men in from the woods to their meals.

The other side of the lumber camp is the bunkhouse. In a crowded camp an unbroken line of rough-boarded double bunks fills each wall. The mattress is a woods spread—a thick padded blanket—and the bedclothes consist of another woods spread. The men crowd together for much-needed warmth, and when one rolls over, his partner must follow suit. Duffel bags and knapsacks full of personal belongings hang on nails over the owner's sleeping place, or from the posts that support the upper bunks. The men wash and shave, if they care to, at a small sideboard near the back door, handy to the open plumbing. A few men build beds of fir boughs on their hard bunks, and use talcum powder profusely and hopefully to keep the lice away.

To bathe in the wintertime is, of course, to commit suicide, and a few put off this distasteful task until their numerous applications of rheumatism liniment finally "smoke" them out in late July, when the rivers and lakes are warm. I once knew a lumberjack who claimed the distinction of never having indulged at all in the mad fashion of bathing. He also said the black flies never bothered him and I wasn't surprised after the sun came out and thawed through his multiple layers of underwear.

Real lumberjacks are not actually so prejudiced against bathing. Once they are out of the woods, they positively glow because of the excessive face scrubbing, haircuts and shaves they indulge in.

Terence F. Harper Collection

A pulpwood pile at Churchill Depot. At the far right is a tractor shed, and second from the right is the blacksmith shop.

A Labrador cruiser, whom I shall call Bill, told me about a lumberjack who wasn't prejudiced against bathing. Bill was in the lobby of a hotel in a small lumber town when the lumberjack approached him from the rear, pounded him on the back, rattled his teeth and bellowed in his ear. "HOLY OLE MACKINAW! Where'd you come from, Bill?"

They exchanged lusty back blows and then Bill followed him upstairs to see a promised eyeful. His friend had engaged a room and a bath! The lumberjack threw the door open, but the room was empty. He went to the bathroom door and opened it with a flourish. "THERE!" he shouted. "What'd I tellya! I'm washing her off a bit!"

In the tub was a wild-eyed half-breed.

The heart of the bunkhouse is the stove, with stockings festooned on a rack over it. The clear space around the stove is the recreation room where the men whittle wooden chains, toys and ax handles, or play poker everlastingly and recklessly. A week's or a month's wages are lost and won during an evening. When too many IOUs pile up against a lumberjack, he "lights out" across country on the longest and farthest-reaching tote road. In small camps, "tailor mades"—manufactured cigarettes—are used as an ante, but even then a carton of cigarettes doesn't last long in a game of Red Dog—that cutthroat bank-roll-busting poker game.

Besides the main camp, if the lumbering operations are on a large scale, there are sheds for horses, tractors, bobsleds, axes, logging chains, crosscut saws, wedges, harnesses and various other pieces of equipment too numerous to mention. There is a small cabin used for an office where the timekeeper reigns supreme. He is an individual very high in the social scale. He reads, writes and keeps the books, sells company supplies to the men, and has his bunk in the office with the woods boss. Cigarettes, plug tobacco, woolen socks, shirts and cotton work gloves are kept on hand to sell to the men. Such supplies are part of the wangan—along with kitchen utensils, blankets and other office equipment. I even knew one old timekeeper who could neither read nor write. He solved his problem most ingeniously. When he sold two plugs of tobacco or a pair of socks, he drew pictures of these articles in the ledger. Then he only had to remember the name of the man who bought them, and what he paid for them.

Chapter 6

Deacon's Seat

I often went down to the Chase Carry camp, hoping for an invitation to eat. The cook there was especially good. The food in camps is usually plentiful and good, and when the men are working hard, four meals a day are served. The camp that serves only baked beans (logging berries) is rare nowadays. Beans are served when the cook and cookees are on the trail with the men following the drive, because they are easier to handle and carry, and they "stick to the ribs." The better camps have ham and eggs for breakfast; meat, potatoes, pea soup and vegetables for dinner; and a hash or baked beans for supper. Tea and coffee are served black, and no meal is complete without cookies, pies and jelly rolls. Lumpy pie filling, crushed and preserved fruits, jamlike raspberry and strawberry, and raisin pie filling are bought by the wooden tubfuls.

The short, chunky cook, completely wrapped in a white apron, appeared in the doorway of the camp. "Mademoiselle, ho got new cookie taday." He held up an enormous molasses cookie. "You like dat. Hi make him for you."

"I'll be right in to eat it, Cook."

41

A lunch was laid on the rough board tables in the kitchen, and cookees were piling up more and more jelly rolls, pies and cakes.

"Enough," I said. "I can't eat all of that!"

"Sure, you heat hall dat. Makes you fat."

They added a bowl of steaming black tea.

Cookees lead a precarious existence. As well as being the butt of every joke in camp, they are blamed for anything that goes wrong in the kitchen. I think that every cookee is credited with having been lost in the woods for three days and of having almost starved to death before being found, still with the two full lunch buckets that he was taking to the men who were too far out to come in to dinner. Cookees are apprentice lumberjacks, and therefore a cookee is experiencing his first winter in the woods. One of the first things he has to learn is how to dry knives, forks and spoons—the correct lumber camp method being to put all such utensils in a bag and shake them dry.

I bit into a jelly roll. "Good jelly roll, Cook. How did you make it?"

The cook blushed with pride. "No heggs."

"No eggs!"

"Sure. Take cup snow for one hegg. You come tomorrow. Hi make big cake same way."

I was doubtful. "I don't know if I'll have time."

"Ho yess. Mans she tell stories." He finished in French to make himself understood. "Tomorrow is Sunday, and there is a man here who is a storyteller. So come tomorrow and listen to him. We have two men here who have accordions too."

I wouldn't have missed that Sunday for anything. The camp storyteller is a popular person, and no crew is complete without one. I remember when I was a youngster we used to gather at a nearby general store that was owned by a lumberman. When the

lumberjacks met there after the drive or before going into the
woods in the early fall, Louie Godin, one such storyteller, would be
pleaded with to repeat his tales. He was a well-educated man
according to woods standards and had read Edgar Rice Burroughs's
Tarzan books. He gave complete chapters from memory, day after
day, with demonstrations and pantomime, swinging from the
beams where hung the pots and pans and hooting realistically
enough to make us believe he was really the "Ape Man." My
brother happened to be picking potatoes one fall on the same farm
with Louie Godin, and during the evening when the men were sitting around the stove in their barracks, Louie would tell them stories. Jack says he thinks that Louie actually repeated word for word
some article on economics that he had read somewhere. It was
weird. Louie Godin was often called the "Pearley Brook Lawyer."

During the two months Louie spent at home, he walked
back and forth to the store every day, and we often saw him surrounded by a group of men, squatting on their heels in the middle of the road and listening to him talk. If cars or teams came
along they had to drive around him, but most of them stopped
to join the group around the storyteller.

The stories were tales of the deeds of old-time lumberjacks,
of their encounters with wolves, bears, bobcats and moose, and I
have heard the wildest tales of a Canada lynx that devoured a
man down to his boot tops, but had to leave the boots because
the leather was too tough. The only genuine Paul Bunyan story I
ever heard was the old one about the cookees who tied salt pork
on the soles of their shoes and skated around on the big frying
pan to grease it for flapjacks. They like stories about the Devil,
or they argue as to whether lice do or don't grow on people.

I thought the French Canadian stories would be much the
same, and usually they are. But this Sunday I received a surprise.

43

The storyteller was a small man who had long since seen sixty years go by. He was seated on a bench near the stove in the bunkhouse with the men grouped around him, sitting on the edges of bunks or on the various benches they call "deacon seats." Why they are called by this name no one knows, but anyway, it's the name that originally was given to the narrow bench that was built from the foot of a bunk to the stove, where the storyteller sat to unfold his yarns.

The story was in French, and I listened, intent on catching every word. He told the story of Cinderella. The names were different but the story was the same. Then he told the story of the Sleeping Beauty. I was astonished.

"You read, Monsieur?" I asked him.

"No, Mademoiselle, I was always sorry I never went to school, but there were no schools."

"Your father told you these stories?" I asked.

"No, my grandfather. He could read and write and was a wonderful storyteller."

We had music the rest of the afternoon. The two boys with the accordions were Allagash boys, and they played and sang cowboy ballads. The majority of lumberjacks have a fondness for ten-gallon hats and the wide, studded belts that the western cowboy is credited with wearing. While I was at Churchill I filled out many order blanks for these hats and belts. The biggest hats and the widest belts with the most stones in them were preferred.

"Give us a dance, Pierre!" someone shouted. Pierre obliged with a clog dance.

The cook was at my elbow. "We got Hallagash mans here can do bear dance. She's bashful. You hask her."

"A bear dance!" I shouted, as anxious as any of them.

After much coaxing a tall, handsome fellow started a "bear" dance, which is really a Russian dance. The dancer squats on his heels, kicks one leg out, jumps and kicks the other leg out, and lands on the alternating foot.

That was one of the most enjoyable afternoons I have ever spent. It was pleasant to be sitting in the open doorway of the lumber camp, getting a look-in at one phase of a lumberjack's life, something few women have the privilege of doing. Neither I nor the men themselves were conscious of the fact that I was the only woman at this stag party. My bulky parka, ski pants and smelly sealskin boots were not exactly glamorous.

The life of a lumberjack sounds picturesque, but it is far from being entirely so. There are the isolation, the long hours of steady work, the hazardous risks and the small amount of pay— a case of the survival of the fittest. As a compensation to those who can stand it, there is the healthy out-of-door life. They rise before daylight, rinse face and hands in icy cold water, file through the dingle—the open shed—into the steamy kitchen, and eat a hearty breakfast with cups and cups of black tea— "sheep-dip," they call it.

The morning is snappy and cold, and the sounds of activities re-echo sharply on the frosty air: the rattling of harnesses and logging chains, sled runners scraping on sparkling snow, axes ringing as they bite deeper and deeper into frozen tree trunks, men shouting and tractors roaring.

The lumberjack is really a mild-mannered fellow, despite his swaggering bluster when he is in civilization. He is sensitive to the attitude of people toward him and will make a special effort to avoid anyone who might snub him. I suppose he has a superiority complex because of the mighty forest monarchs he has subdued. The wide-open spaces will develop a wide-open personality.

Many of the lumberjacks have families and homes. Some are farmers who have had an unfortunate bout with Lady Luck and have had to supplement the family income by working "in the woods," but the real "Timber Wolf" is generally a bachelor. He has always been a lumberjack and always will be. He drifts from camp to camp, spending his holidays and wages on Hancock Street in Bangor, for tomorrow he may be heading back to the woods. As far as work is concerned, there isn't much difference between the lumberjack and his employer: the lumberjack works all winter cutting down trees and when spring comes he spends all his money in one grand splurge; the employer works to get all his trees cut and then has to wait another hundred years for them to grow up again.

The lumberjack is the main cog in the lumber industry. He chooses a tree, undercuts it on the side he wishes it to fall, and starts to saw opposite the notch. He wedges the tree as it starts to pinch, limbs and tops it as it lies on the ground. His work is hard and the hours long. When the lumberjack is through with a log and it is ready to be taken away, a chain is looped around one end and tightened, and the log is hauled by a horse on the narrow "twitching" paths that lead to loading yards on the hauling road. The logs are piled on the side of the road to be loaded onto bobsleds—double sleds, two sleds or wagon sleds, as they are variously called—that carry them to the landing on the river.

The hauling road—or wagon sled road—is broad and smooth and is constantly being repaired and improved to keep the heavy loads from slipping off. It is tended by "road monkeys" or "chickadees"—a crew of men who keep it iced in the wintertime so the steel sled runners will slide easily. Logs are handled by men with cant dogs, spiked bars with a dog—a loose, curved hook—on the end of it. The dog tightens on a log when pressure is exerted, and the log is easily rolled by the leverage action of the bar. The cant dog is a Maine invention. In the old days a handspike was used—the same bar with a loose dog that had to be tightened by hand with a ring that fitted over it and held it there. A man in Brewer, Maine, who was named Peavey, invented the socket for the dog, and it was called a peavey, but more often a cant dog.

The main yarding spot is on the bank of a river. Logs are piled on this landing twenty and thirty feet high with a par-buckle—a common crane. A scaler measures the logs for the exact number of board feet.

Chapter 7

Wilderness Airways

Anna called me from my room one day. "There is a man down here who wants to see you."

I went down and met one of the men from a back camp. "I'm from Fort Kent," he introduced himself, "and I wonder if you would call Portage on the telephone and have them send a plane in."

I didn't stop to ask why, but when the message had been delivered, I turned to him. "What seems to be the trouble?"

"One of my friends cut his knee."

"Why don't you bring him in here and we'll take a look at it?"

I had no intention of playing doctor, but a little first aid might help. The man, really a boy of seventeen, limped into the living room. Anna and I unwrapped the dirty, blood-soaked rags from around his knee, cleaned the wound as well as we could, and wrapped clean strips of sheeting around it. The plane came for him an hour later and the men carried him down on the ice, boarded the plane and took off. A week later his buddy came back. We learned that the boy would recover but wouldn't be able to work that winter. He could thank his lucky stars that there were such things as airplanes.

Accidents in the camps are not as common as would be supposed. The men are woodsmen and know how to handle an ax, and it is only due to freaks of nature or carelessness that they get hurt. Trees freeze as hard as iron in the wintertime, and even the sharpest ax will make little headway. A loose, carelessly held ax will skewer sideways with a surprising, twisting force.

There are many home remedies for infected cuts, colds and rheumatism, which are the three major complaints. The rind of a piece of salt pork placed over a festered cut will draw out the poison. Mustard plasters—dry mustard, flour and water—are an old standby for a chest cold. I lay in bed for three days once at Churchill with a chest cold. I balked at the castor oil. "I won't take any of that stuff," I told Anna. "The cold is in my chest."

She brought up a mustard plaster. "Try this anyway, and don't be so stubborn."

I submitted to it, and all I can say is—it works. But don't keep it on too long!

Every lumberjack has rheumatism at some time in his life, and there are surprisingly few painkillers for it. The most popular pill in lumber camps is aspirin from the wangan.

Tobacco juice is often used as an antiseptic for sore eyes, and blowing smoke in an ear for an earache really does relieve the pain. The queerest one I ever heard was the old French Canadian superstition that piercing the ear lobes, as if for earrings, will cure sore or weak eyes.

If anyone wants to get out in a hurry, the best way, and the quickest, is by plane. But a plane can't always land in the woods—never during freeze-up or spring break-up. One could board the train at Lac Frontiere for a roundabout trip to nowhere, but the railroad ended at Lac Frontiere, which is a good jumping-off place.

The north woods pilots were a devil-may-care crew who made their living flying over this vast, silent and lonely area of timberland. They flew through unpredictable weather conditions, guided hunters and fishermen to remote and desolate sportsmen's paradises, and ferried men back and forth to the lumber camps. They brought in fur dealers and supplies to wilderness cabins, and rescued solitary trappers who were getting woods queer, mumbling to themselves, starting at the sound of a twig snapping, and imagining gruesome horrors on a lost, uncharted and godforsaken lake.

Their Taylor Cubs, Stinsons and old Curtis Robins were dilapidated, drafty and overloaded, but they were ready for any emergency. To some lonely hermit who was sick or hurt, depressed and weary of the solitary life, or just deliriously happy to see anyone, they were Apollo in his Golden Chariot. If they said they would be there sometime, they were late. But if they were needed in a hurry, they were Johnny on the spot.

I remember the woods boss who broke his back in one of the camps. A Portage pilot landed on a little mud pond that no self-respecting plane could pancake onto. He flew the man out, saving a life at the risk of his own.

I remember the two old cronies living on Musquacook Lake who couldn't wait for a springtime spree, but decided to have it then and there. One of the pair called Portage to say that Dave was dying in his arms, and to bring in some whisky, and "For God's sake, hurry!"

Dave was very much alive and was impatiently running out on the ice when the rescue ship landed.

And a year later when a similar call came into Portage via the network of forest telephone lines, the pilot never hesitated about going. Dave was really dying.

We knew most of the pilots by their first names. Jerry Smead was considered the best. He was the pilot who could pancake onto a mud pond and take off again, and he was also credited with one of the closest shaves and some of the fastest thinking ever heard of in that country. Jerry was notoriously absentminded and always thrilled his passengers by picking up one of his western books that he carried with him and proceeding to read while flying. He looked like one of Zane Grey's heroes. One day while taking off from Portage Lake, Jerry had barely started to climb when the unpredictable motor in his unpredictable ship coughed twice and died. The passenger found himself staring at a string of telephone wires. The ship dipped under the wires, the motor caught, and Jerry zoomed up again, banking between two houses. Within three seconds Jerry had picked up his book and was "out on the range" again.

And then there was Bud McKinney who was handsome and debonair, and who would just as soon fly over that country at night as in the daytime. He landed on Churchill a good many moonlit nights with no landing flares to guide him in. Bud was a good pilot but he couldn't drive a car. He started out from Churchill one time with a borrowed car, and two hours later Bud walked into the settlement. The car was out in the woods.

There was also a small, dark fellow from the south who had never seen snow until he came to Maine. He kept picking up handfuls of it to inspect it. And there was Seth who surpassed all of them for sheer recklessness. Many a startled family at Churchill has suddenly evacuated their dwelling place thinking that Seth had this time misjudged the distance between his landing skis and the roof of their house. Seth was always out of funds and gasoline. He left Churchill one day for Portage with a tankful of low-grade gasoline, which is really a high-grade kerosene that the lumber company sold at fourteen cents a gallon. He later paid for the gasoline by giving the blacksmith flying lessons.

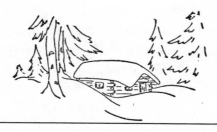

Chapter 8

Halfway to Nowhere

I had been at Churchill for six months, and at Easter time I decided to spend my vacation downriver. Despite the adventurous novelty of living at Churchill, the long winter months did grow dull and monotonous and I thought spring would never come. It didn't seem possible that there could be so much snow in one winter. I had seen a lot of snow in the St. John Valley, and some snowdrifts that were twenty and thirty feet high on the Madawaska-Van Buren road. But it was depressing to know that for miles and miles around there was this heavy, white blanket shutting us in, with a little moth hole for Churchill. I was glad when we walked down on the ice to the plane. The pilot noticed my smile.

"Glad you're going out?" he asked.

"You bet!"

"Ever flown before?"

"Just twice, and those rides were so short they didn't count."

The first time I had seen an airplane was when a barnstorming trio had landed in Pete Daigle's field in Fort Kent. I was eleven years old, and like everyone else in town, I spent my time on Pete's woodpile behind the barn watching the performance. The ship was an open one, and we oh'ed and ah'ed expecting him to fall out when he stunted over the field. Rides were five dollars, and I could only look. The woman parachuted and I fell in love with the wing walker. It is too bad we have to grow up and step casually into a plane with no illusion left of riding on the clouds.

It was cold and slightly cloudy the afternoon we left Churchill—John, the same lumberjack I had seen in such a battered condition that first day at Churchill, Bud, the pilot, and myself. We taxied up the lake, and with a feeling that the plane was being lifted by wires, we took off and circled Churchill.

The settlement was insignificant compared to the uninterrupted forest surrounding it—farther than the eye could see. Twitching roads and hauling roads from the back camps looked like spokes of a wheel, with the landing as the hub. A Lombard with a trail of loaded bobsleds crawled over a tiny line, and as we swung off across country, it was suddenly shut off as though it had disappeared behind a hill.

It is about fifty miles across to Portage Lake as the crow flies, with nothing in between—no people, no habitation, no roads—nothing but what seemed like a thousand lakes and ponds. There was no greeting line of smoke rising toward us from deserted, tumbledown and snow-mantled camps and cabins. From the air the country is naked in the wintertime, with no foliage to hide the humiliating sight of former logging operations.

After the stormy and rough height of land around the four Musquacook lakes, the land is rolling and almost level. It began to snow, and the large flakes flying by the window soon shut off the view. The plane circled and landed on McNally Pond, only halfway to our destination but a safe port in a storm.

As we stepped from the plane, the storm closed around us, an icy cold and freezing blizzard swirling in cloudy mists, first curtaining the shore and then disclosing it. I shivered in my silly skirt and silk stockings, wishing I hadn't been so anxious for the first touch of civilization. We were stranded and might be there three or four days if the storm didn't let up. One might just as well be at the North Pole at that time of year as at McNally Pond.

The pilot bedded his plane for the night, shouting above the blowing gale. "There's a camp about two miles . . ." the wind carried away the rest of his explanation and he shouted louder ". . . by the old wooden dam."

He led the way down the old tote road and we wallowed, fell, struggled and sluggishly pushed forward through six feet of snow, sinking to our waists. On the marsh the going was better, and we only sank to our knees. The wet snow under the protecting top crust was not frozen, and we sloshed and slushed through it. The sharp crust made short work of my stockings, and my legs were covered with scratches. I was soon crawling on my hands and knees so I wouldn't sink in the frigid water. It was the longest two miles I ever walked—hound dog miles: they run a hound dog to death in the woods and call it a mile.

The cabin at the dam was buried in snow. It was ramshackle and solitary, with an open lean-to shed seemingly supporting it and a rakish eye-winking tilt to one corner of the porch roof. We crawled up the bank and over the mound of drifted snow that semicircled the front of it, pushed open the door and walked in, peering into the unaccustomed darkness.

"There's no stove!" John exclaimed.

"Should be an oil-barrel stove here. It must be in the dingle." Bud went outside to rummage among the heaped objects in the lean-to, brushed off a covering of snow and discovered a stove, a few lengths of pipe and an elbow. It was a "haywire outfit"—a real Maine invention. The backwoods people quickly recognized the enormous possibilities of haywire for repairing broken-down machinery and for building their primitive "contraptions." Hence the term "haywire outfit." This stove was hung together and operated with looped pieces of wire, but we set it up, stuck the chimney out of a window and soon had a fire going with old chips and boards. We huddled around the heat, thawing, dripping and trying to grin. Curiously, none of us talked much and no mention was made of our predicament. I was too busy trying to think of a substitute for shoes and stockings, in case we had to walk out of there. My bare legs tingled.

In one corner of the camp was a bunk covered with damp, moldy straw, shreds of patched and mildewed blankets, and old clothes. In the opposite corner was a stack of filthy, discarded rags, an occasional half-raveled stocking, a dirt-stiffened pant leg, and a moths' nest of old woolen shirts. It was a solution to the stocking problem.

Battered plates, tin cups and a spider were still on a sideboard, left unwashed after the last meal eaten there. John found a kerosene lamp and Bud melted snow water to wash the dishes. I found one cup of sour-smelling buckwheat flour, a handful of barley and a small piece of crusty salt pork. It was unappetizing but we were hungry enough to eat "boiled bum." We had boiled barley, fried salt pork and a makeshift pancake for supper.

"I'd just as lief have chicken," John said. "Or how about a juicy sirloin served on a hot platter?"

"We'll probably be eating porcupine tomorrow, if one is foolish enough to come out of his den. I'm not going to leave the dishes unwashed this time." I was pessimistic. The gloomy cabin and howling wind outside were too real to laugh at.

Bud was more cheerful. "If we can't get out of here tomorrow I'll start for the Musquacooks to get us some grub. I know Dave Howe has some."

"A little matter of twenty miles to nowhere," I said. "If anyone ever sees me stepping into a plane again with silk stockings and a skirt on, I hope they kick me good and hard."

We spent the rest of the evening playing cards, but the only game we could play was rummy. Someone had been playing poker and a full house—three aces and a pair of tens—was missing.

About ten o'clock the weather cleared and the temperature started to drop. The sky was a deep blue and high up, and the curtains of northern lights danced and flickered in an unending stream across the heavens. Watching them steadily gives the impression that they are crackling or rustling like taffeta, and the closer they are, the louder the rustle.

"We can fly out now," Bud said.

"How about the motor," John asked. "Will it start?"

"Dunno. It might. Must be thirty below zero now."

"Might just as well stay here," I said. "I'd hate to go over that trek twice in case it didn't. Anyway, we can get out in the morning."

We had collected enough wood for the night, and after the breath of fresh air, we turned back to the musty, warm cabin. I was given the choice of any sleeping quarters, but since the bench was too short and the bunk too disreputable looking, I pulled a long board up to the stove and lay down for a winter's nap. Bud sprawled amid the moldy straw.

There is nothing in the world as hard to sleep on as a board, especially if one is restless and wakeful—and not well padded. I wriggled and squirmed, trying to keep on the darn thing, resting my head first on one arm, then on the other. I got splinters in my legs and one in my chin. Then the fun started when I started scratching. I pulled up my parka hood and tightened it but it was too late. The place was literally lousy. I could hear John scratching and muttering about the "Jeesley cooties!" before he fell off his narrow bench, gave it up as a bad job, and crawled onto the bunk too.

The night grew colder and the lice grew bolder, and I—less fastidious now—joined the two on the bunk. I shook Bud. "Push over," I said. "I want to sleep in the middle."

Bud rolled over. "Huh," he grunted, then his eyes opened. "*What*! Oh yes, yeah—" He was asleep again. We slept fitfully, waking to put more wood in the stove and to scratch the persistent lice. We were up at dawn watching the glow in the east with the temperature down to forty below zero.

By eight o'clock the sky was bright and clear, and we waited two more hours, hoping the sun would warm the plane enough so Bud could start it. The crust had frozen as hard as iron, and we walked along easily where we had floundered so the day before. The morning was nippy, but the March sun was warm. Bud didn't have a "firepot"—an overgrown blowtorch—to warm the engine with, and he and John took turns swinging the propeller. In an hour we taxied around the little pond before taking off.

As we flew into Portage, the first signs of civilization I noticed were snowshoe tracks, which are so distinct from the air. The sight of black tarred roads leading everywhere seemed unbelievable after Churchill. Just as the plane taxied to a stop on shore, I heard the whistle of the train going to Fort Kent and I raced pell-mell after it, boarded it as it left the station, and headed for the washroom to take off a layer of grease and grime and straighten my hair.

The car wasn't crowded, but the few passengers eyed me queerly. The conductor was curious. "Just come out of the woods?"

"I think it is quite obvious." I chased *Pediculus capitis* up the back of my neck and scratched like blue blazes when I had him cornered.

"You can sit in the smoker. Most of the lumberjacks do."

"Listen—I'll have you know I am a respectable school-teacher." (Though you'd never have known it to look at me.)

He laughed. "I was only kidding. Where did you come out, back of Ashland?"

"Way back. Churchill, to be exact."

On that short visit outside I really appreciated things I had taken for granted. I drank chocolate sodas at the drugstore, ate crabmeat and lettuce sandwiches at the corner lunch stand, played the jukebox, and saw everyone I knew. I surprised Great-grandma with my collection of French idioms, although she was quite familiar with most of them. I was quite satisfied with a week of it, however, and was glad to get back to Churchill, this time without mishap.

Chapter 9

River Drive

The settlement was as quiet as a church. Work had slowed down as most of the long lumber was piled on the landing, waiting for the ice to go out. Everybody seemed to be waiting. There was an expectation in the air—not a tension, but no plans were made for the morrow.

One morning I awoke and my room was warm. A soft, wet-smelling breeze came through the partly open window, and I could hear water dripping from the eaves. Spring was here and even the kitchen noises were louder and happier. The lake ice was grayish, as the ice softened and water seeped through. The river ice was bluish in patches. Trees were darker, glistening wet from the melting ice that had coated them.

During the next two days the snow melted fast, running in little brooks and standing in puddles in the road, pouring down the riverbank and gurgling under the snow. All day and during the quiet reading hours at school I heard the *swoosh* and *plop-plop* of breaking icicles and sliding snow on the roof of the cabin. The yards around the houses were bare as the escaping heat from inside the houses pushed back the snow and the accumulation of dust and debris began to show through.

The back camps were closed and the men moved into Churchill to wait for the "drive." Many of them made short visits to their homes, and some returned with permanent waves and a few more gold teeth. The permanent waves were fuzzy and funny, but curly hair is the height of range-road beauty. The gold teeth were an investment and a mark of distinction. If you could afford gold teeth, then you were a man of means.

And of course there is the old, old story about Joe.

Joe she's come hout de woods, hongries jus lak a bar. Hall winter Joe she's heat same ting hevery day, and dats beans and *soupe au poi*. She's go to café hon top of Fort Kent and by gar she's tink dats someting nize. He's no heat same ting here. He's horder de ting she's cost do mose. De firs ting Joe get, she's bowl pea soup. Joe she's look hat dat. She's say, "By gar! Pea soup, where you pass me hon de tote road?"

With so many quick-tempered and hotheaded lumberjacks at the boardinghouse, the bar-r-room was noisy. Mr. Deblois was well known for his pugilistic abilities in his younger days and was still respected for it, but he was busy keeping peace. For a man who had been severely injured from a fall that broke his back, "The Bull of the Woods" could still bounce the rowdies around, taking them by the collar and the seat of the pants and tossing them through the door for a free ride.

One casualty appeared at the table, somewhat subdued, with his features battered beyond recognition. It was "Pickles," an especially mouthy individual, whose bunk companions had apparently gone to work on him with caulked boots. There are no rules or ethics in lumberjack fighting. You can use caulked boots as well as your hands.

When the fast-melting snow and small brooks swelled the river, breaking away the imprisoning ice in a grinding roar, the exuberant energies of the men were diverted to the drive. Whooping and shouting like Indians on a warpath, they tore down to the landing at Chase Carry. News that the ice was going out spread through the settlement like wildfire, and those who could leave went down to see it go. I hurriedly declared a recess from school and raced after them.

The men were breaking out the landing, crawling like flies over the enormous mass of piled timbers, picking out key logs and letting others roll down into the angry, turbulent spring freshet. Cant dogs flew at top speed, and forty-foot timbers tossed and danced in the whitewater. Big *bateaus* were launched and ran the rapids on Devil's Elbow that no canoe would have lived through.

Cook nudged my elbow. "See Ferguson?"

"Who's Ferguson?"

"Big mans wit de gray hair."

"I've been watching him. What's he standing on the landing for?"

Cook looked owlishly wise and made a circular motion around his ear. "Crazee old river hog. She's ride de logs. Quick! I tell you!"

The man we had been talking about leaped from his perch as a huge log sailed by him. He landed like a cat and both feet flashed as the log spun and twisted over the rolling swells.

"Yippee!" he shouted. "Stay with her, Ferguson! You gray-headed old son of a whore! Hold her out where she's white and foamy!"

The drive moved downriver with the men following—wading, riding the long lumber, or walking along the driver's path that followed the river to the drive's destination. They pushed along the stragglers that were caught in a backwash of current, or loosened those that were caught in midstream on rocks and sandbars, and they were ever alert for the dangers of a jam.

A log jam is a common and extremely dangerous occurrence. In their speedy flight on the fast-moving water, thirty-foot timbers toss and tumble like matchsticks in the capricious river and pile up hurriedly around any obstruction. They interweave and tighten, and steadily gather more timbers behind it to reach higher and higher. The water is dammed until the force of pressure sometimes releases the jam in a terrific, pounding cataclysm. Sometimes a jam has to be dynamited, and the man who walks out to set the charge and light the fuse under the head of the jam faces death. At any moment the slightest jar may start it moving and bury him under an avalanche of crushing timbers. Small jams may be released by hand, by picking out the key logs and freeing the others.

The cook, the cookees and the grub wagons followed the drive down the river, serving four meals a day in the open air. When the drive went through Umsaskis Lake, valuable time was lost because the wind wasn't blowing in the right direction to carry the lumber toward the outlet. A boom was used—a series of logs chained together and enclosing the lumber to keep it from escaping. Motorboats towed the boom down to the outlet.

There are many kinds of booms to serve their various purposes. *Shear booms* are used on a river to cut off a cove or inlet where the backwash of a current would bottle up the logs. Both ends of a shear boom are hooked to the riverbank or piers. A *fin boom* is used for the same purpose, but only one end is anchored on shore while the current holds the other end in place. *Bathurst booms* are squared and placed one on top of the other, and are used for booming pulp wood, to keep the pulp from slipping under. Booms and piers are strung across a river to stop a drive at its destination—a sawmill or a railroad loading station.

Churchill was left in peace and quiet. The lake ice broke away from the shores, was pounded by conflicting winds and disappeared. A week later, "King" La Croix unexpectedly closed his lumber camps. One by one the families packed and moved away, some going back to Canada, and some to the United States to apply for naturalization papers. My pupils drifted away and I was alone, sorting books, papers, chalk, pens and pencils, thinking that this school, as well as the settlement, would never open again.

The day may come when isolated lumber camps and river drives will be seen no more in Maine. Even the lumberjacks may become legendary figures who wore funny spiked boots and checkered shirts. When conservation replaces the robber-baron tactics of landowners and "big lumber men," perhaps the great-great-grandchildren of this generation will once more know the forests of our grandfathers. But they will never know the lumberjack as we know him, because he is a product of his time. I can't imagine a cookee "pot walloping" with an electrical dishwasher.

Churchill Depot is almost another lumber camp ghost settlement. Porcupines have taken up their abode in the back camps. The garage, office, sawmill, blacksmith shop and stables are deserted. There were but three families left at Churchill—a scaler's family, a trapper's family and La Croix's caretakers at the boardinghouse.

It was with a real sense of loss that I boarded the train at Monk, Canada, for a long, bumpy, night ride to Fort Kent. I knew I'd be back. Curly, the game warden at Umsaskis, and I were going to be married that fall.

Chapter 10
Warden's Wife

I had been at Churchill a week when a delegation of five game wardens appeared at the boardinghouse for dinner. They were much too carefully groomed to be on the trail of a poacher. During dinner I tried hard to appear unimpressed with these snappily uniformed "arms of the law." Their grayish-blue pants with a black stripe down the side and their dark coats with Sam Browne belts and holsters are exactly what you think the well-dressed forest ranger should wear. At that time game wardens were also wearing campaign hats, and they were much more glamorous than the officers' caps they wear now. I didn't miss Leon Wilson's slick black hair, Hallie Dow's witty remarks, or the high polish on Dave Jackson's badge and belt.

When I stepped out of the boardinghouse to go over to school, there they were, all sitting on a log in front of the building. I started for the school, and for some unknown reason I turned around quickly and caught them staring. I stuck my tongue out at them and hurried on.

They guffawed. One of them fell off the log, and Leon Wilson hooted, "My God, Curly, you don't have to break a leg now. You're the only one that can squire her around this winter."

I could have killed the darn fools.

When I spent a weekend with Mr. and Mrs. Wilson on the St. John River, I was formally introduced to Mr. Hamlin, better known as Curly.

One Saturday he called at the boardinghouse and asked if I cared to go partridge hunting. The next day he brought me some magazines, and three days later he called at the boardinghouse with Levi Dow, warden supervisor from Fort Kent. Everyone who has been in the Maine woods either knows Levi Dow or has heard of him. He is a legendary woodsman, and his fund of stories is unequaled. I was invited to a partridge feed at the Umsaskis camp.

Levi still insists that I ate four partridges that night, three sweet potatoes, a dozen biscuits, and four cups of coffee. Mr. Hamlin and I reached the "Curly" and "Helen" stage. I was invited to go partridge hunting on Saturday, and I accepted.

From then on the sledding was easy. We were in love. Of course we were as circumspect and reticent as was to be expected. We did manage to hold hands when we went out to play cards with the postmistress and her husband, and had to get kicked on the shins whenever it was time to bid. I did get in dutch one time, and I must tell this on myself. It is too good to keep.

We had gone to a dance at Lac Frontiere. Curly was to drive me back to Churchill, and we didn't leave the party until the last fiddle was packed in its case. We drove slowly, and you know how time flies. Dawn was breaking before we were halfway there.

I was suddenly aware of the lateness of the hour. "What time is it?"

"Five-thirty in the morning."

"That late? I can't be seen driving into Churchill with you at this hour! What will everybody say?"

"Why don't you stay at my camp tonight," Curly suggested. "I can drive you up tomorrow, or today rather, and maybe they'll think you stayed at Clayton or something."

That "or something" didn't sound just right, but it seemed better than my stepping out of the game warden's car when everyone else was waking up. I agreed, and we drove into his camp on Umsaskis. He generously offered me the couch in the kitchen and a pair of his pajamas, and he slept in the back bedroom.

I must have been dozing but a short while when he shook me awake. "Better get up. There's a plane landing on the ice!"

I was wide awake. "Who is it?"

"I forgot to tell you. Some friends of mine were here yesterday and they said they would be back." He had his pants and a sweater on, and a pair of sealskin boots on his bare feet.

I clutched the overgrown pajamas to keep them from falling off, dove out of bed, grabbed my clothes and headed for the back bedroom to dress. He locked the door behind me.

I don't remember to this day how I dressed as quickly as I did, or how I ever managed to unlock the door with a coat hanger, but by the time the "company" was stepping onto the porch, I had combed my hair and was building a fire in the stove. I heard Curly outside, talking much too loudly to sound natural.

"I just went up to Churchill for the schoolteacher!"

My ears are burning now, but at the time I really wanted to laugh. It had snowed that morning and there wasn't a track around the camp. I'm sure I don't know what those people thought, but I'll bet it wasn't complimentary. Curly did say later that I looked as though I had just stepped out of a bandbox. I felt as though I had stepped from something less tidy.

The next weekend when Anna said, "That man is here again," I growled. "Tell him I don't want to see him. My good reputation is in shreds already. Where is he?"

"He's in the kitchen eating cookies. I guess he has Mrs. Bridges with him for a chaperone."

It wasn't lonesomeness in a wilderness that brought us together, or that our temperaments are alike. We both wanted the same kind of a life and were headstrong enough to get it. I like the woods and so does Curly. Curly is a tall, broad-shouldered woodsman, with a square jaw and clear blue eyes. (A sportswoman once remarked to me, "Your husband is just too-o-o stunning!" It took me a week to bring Curly back to earth!)

I think every wife likes to talk about her courtship. I am no exception. The day we were to be married, Curly drove through Canada to Fort Kent, had two flat tires on the way, and a third when he reached town. He had to buy a new tire. We drove to a town in the Province of New Brunswick, hoping we could be married the same day, since he had to go back to work as soon as possible.

A minister informed us that we would have to wait five days, and when we told him the circumstances, he suggested we drive to another town to see a judge who might waive the five-day law.

The next day we drove to a Canadian town to see the judge, and he and Curly went into consultation. At first he wasn't sure that we were really free, white and twenty-one, but when Curly pulled imposing documents out of his pockets, including a permit from the Royal Canadian Mounted Police to carry a gun in Canada, the judge was impressed. He waived the law.

We drove back to the minister, had two more flat tires, and bought another tire.

Photo courtesy of Dean B. Bennett

Umsaskis Lake.

The minister asked Curly, "Do you take this woman to be your lawful wedded wife?"

"Oh, yeah," he answered. He swears he didn't, but I insist he did. Anyway, at last we were married, and we drove back to Fort Kent.

"My gosh!" Curly came to life. "Dave Daigle promised me two bags of potatoes!"

I was ready for anything. "Turn the car around and we'll go after them."

Dave Daigle was in bed, but he informed us through an open window that the potatoes were already dug; we would find bags in the barn and we could help ourselves. We picked potatoes. The ground was muddy and my new shoes were ruined, but we filled two bags, loaded them into the car, and started for Umsaskis.

Within three hundred yards we had another flat tire. This was ceasing to be funny. The garage was still open, and we had the tire fixed.

We drove all night, taking turns at the wheel and ministering to our dog. We had no more flat tires and we arrived at Umsaskis at six o'clock in the morning. I was dozing on the seat and Curly shook me awake. "We've got another flat tire!"

"No!" I bolted upright.

"So help me, we really have!" It was the seventh flat tire!

In September we were back at Umsaskis. Our home was a two-room log camp overlooking the lake, facing the early-morning sun and shaded by tall, black-striped birches. The roof of the camp was built of cedar splits, massive shingles that are split by hand from a dry, straight-grained cedar. The garage was completely finished with these same cedar splits, but they were older than the ones on the camp. The springhouse behind the camp was comparatively new and was built of small logs. We had an outhouse, a two-seater that was painted a bottle green. During the summer we could sit there and slap mosquitoes, and during the winter we could sit and shiver. A Fish and Game sign hung on the door, and it proclaimed to the world: FLY FISHING ONLY.

Curly had planted a hodgepodge garden that spring, and it had turned out surprisingly well. Under each hill of corn he buried a few chub—a type of perch—and he had the best and only corn in the country. At the old lumber camp on Drake Brook he had scattered a few squash seeds back of the hovel, and that fall we harvested thirty squash. It never happened again because the porcupines always ate them.

I liked the Umsaskis camp. The logs were golden colored, and a raftered ceiling rose to a peak of mellowed cedar splits. The cookstove was tiny, but a bulldog stove furnished our heat.

Photo courtesy of Dean B. Bennett

Umsaskis Lake.

There were cupboards and a small sideboard with a wooden sink. We had a dozen earthenware plates, half a dozen coffee mugs, tin pans, knives, forks, spoons, tin cups, a coffee pot, two kettles, a baker sheet and an assortment of glasses—mustard glasses, jelly glasses and small cheese glasses.

The camp was small and the scarcity of furniture seemed unimportant. Either Curly or the Fish and Game Department had a fondness for the bottle-green paint that was in evidence, but I soon changed it for something cream colored from a mail-order catalogue.

The bedroom had been added after the main part of the camp was built, and it was low ceilinged and quite dark. Curly had it cluttered with gasoline cans, outboard motors, carpenter's tools, hawsers, chains and all the rest of the impedimenta a game warden picks up and carries around with him.

I went into the bedroom at night with a sense of apprehension. I peered into the darkness, trying hard to remember what it was that Curly had brought home today. Was it the roll of sheathing paper, or was it the wash boiler that had only one hole in it? No, that was last night I fell in the wash boiler. Well, here goes. I threw caution to the winds, stepped forward bravely, stubbed my toe on the propeller of a motor, upset the gasoline cans, and rolled over them. I bumped my head on a piece of stovepipe and stuck my other foot into a pan of turpentine and paintbrushes. I was then close enough to the bed to make a leap for it.

I leaped. I landed. And I swore like a lumberjack.

Curly bounced up. "Now what's the matter?"

"Light a match, quick! I'm lost! This used to be the bed but it feels like cardboard."

"My boxes! You're squashing my boxes!"

"Boxes! Oh lord! But I'm supposed to sleep here!"

"I just got them today and I forgot to move them. You women make more fuss; and don't lose my new inner tube."

"Inner tube!"

"You've got it around your neck. Now don't go moving things around or I'll never be able to find anything. Can't you go to bed at night without stewing about it?"

There was a lot of work to be done before cold weather set in, and since we would be marooned through the winter, we had to plan five or six months ahead. Curly hired two Indians from Daaquam to cut five cords of stove wood. The price was a dollar a cord, and when they brought a load of wood into camp, he noticed that there was only a cord and a half.

"When are you going to haul the rest?" he asked.

They looked blank, and I was called to interpret.

"No more, no more. Das hall," they vigorously declared.

"But this is only a cord and a half."

"No, no, fi' cord'." They shook their heads and waved their arms.

We all talked at once.

A gleam of intelligence showed in their brown eyes. "Ho yess, *grosse corde*," they pointed to Curly. "*Face corde*." They thumped their chests. Meaning that what Curly had wanted was full cords, and what they thought he wanted was face cords, a third of a full cord.

We all grinned and Curly ordered ten more "cords." A dollar a cord had sounded rather inexpensive.

The first job we had to do was to chink the camp and put quarter round—small quartered logs—on the inside. It wasn't the right time of year to peel quarter round, so we went across the lake to the old Cunliff camps for secondhand pieces and portaged it across the lake. I think it was more of a job to rip it off the old camps than it would have been to cut it. We measured, sawed, straightened old nails, pounded and broke a lamp chimney, and by the time we reached the bedroom, there wasn't enough quarter round to finish the job. We just filled in the biggest spaces.

The quarter round made a noticeable difference in the warmth of the camp, and with only a small fire in the cookstove, we opened the door to let in the cool, early-fall air. The radio was turned on and the gasoline lantern hissed. We could hear water whispering on the shore of the lake, and the loons—*medawisla*, the Indians named them—mournfully calling for wind. Leaves swished in the light breeze and a cricket chirped under the porch steps.

The rough board wood box showed up like a sore toe in all the glory of "new" quarter round, and the next day Curly cruised the back ridge for birch trees, peeled the bark off in four-foot strips and covered the wood box. I painted an Indian head on the bark. Birch bark takes oil nicely. The grain of the bark shows through but is really attractive. I had enough bark left over to make a large State of Maine seal to hang over the desk, a few Christmas cards, and thin sheets of stationery and envelopes. If one goes over the birch bark with an eraser, it is easily and attractively painted with watercolors. A pinecone and branch or an Indian canoe or a headdress are decorative as letterheads, and sewing the envelopes with colored thread and a blanket stitch makes them firm and woodsy looking.

The cupboards were askew and Curly straightened them, building new doors on some and fitting in pieces of board on those around the sink where the floor had heaved. He built an extension sideboard, extra shelves in the bedroom for groceries and our personal belongings, and a closet for our clothes. His progress was hindered by a collection of saws, hammers, cans of nails, square, plane, awl, and odds and ends of lumber in the middle of the floor.

"Hold this for me," he struggled with a board, "while I put a nail in."

"It doesn't fit."

"Yes, it does. I measured it."

"No, it doesn't. You come see."

"Well, I'll be damned. I forgot to measure the width of the board. Now I'll have to go down to the lumber camp again and get another table."

"La Croix will have you in the hoosegow," I warned.

"I'll shovel the roof off for him next winter."

That's the way they live in that country.

The day my trunk came was the day the chimney was cleaned. While unpacking all the unnecessary finery and feminine folderols to find my blue jeans, woolen shirt and moccasins, Curly tapped the stovepipe to shake down the soot. He pulled the elbow loose to spoon it out, lost his balance when the chair collapsed, and came down in a black cloud. He fell in the sink and kicked over the water pail.

"My dress!" I howled. "My new pink dress!"

"Don't say a word, Pooie," Curly gingerly climbed out of the sink. "I'll buy you another one. Let's call it a day and go swimming."

Curly had once asked me what a louse was in French. I told him it was *pou*.

"Poo," he said. "Poo, poo, pooie. Silly."

Now he calls me Pooie because he likes the sound of it.

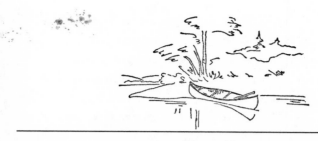

Chapter 11

Buck Fever

Life wasn't all carpentry and ashes. Fall is the best time of year, and September fishing can't be beaten. Every evening found us on our way to the head of the lake with the outboard motor purring and the canoe riding level on a mirror surface. Fly rods were ready and we were warmly dressed for the cold ride home. The trout pool, where a limit of brook trout was waiting for us, was in the large bog at the inlet of the Allagash River.

When we were quiet, deer came down to the bank to drink. I first noticed them watching us suspiciously with only their heads showing through the branches. Then a large buck and two does curiously and timidly advanced to stand silhouetted against a black and gold sunset.

"Shh," I whispered to Curly. "See the deer."

"I know, I heard them. Beauties, aren't they?"

A breeze marred the glassy lake as the sun sank behind the dark spruces. "Reel in. Time to go." Curly laid down his rod and wound the starting rope around the motor. We left the bogan and the deer still standing on the narrow strip of sandbar, undisturbed by our trespassing.

When the season for hunting partridge—ruffed grouse—
opened, we dined well, shooting them according to need while
driving along the road. The few hunters that get up that far
know that when I say partridges are plentiful, I'm not exagger-
ating. Only a small number of partridges are seen on the road,
but even then it looks like a hen yard when a flock of twelve or
fourteen are out scratching for gravel. Partridges, fried in salt-
pork fat, golden and brown flecked, white and tender inside,
and served with sweet potatoes, are among the most delicious
treats in the world. We baked them in a bean pot, had them in
stews with dumplings, or in a pie with a biscuit crust. Spruce
partridge, a darker variety of ruffed grouse, is mistakenly
shunned by some hunters, but preferred by those who know
how tasty they are when baked with beans.

On the first day of open season at Umsaskis, I went partridge hunting alone. I knew the difference between a shotgun
and a rifle, and the fine points about hunting—don't look down
the muzzle and pull the trigger to see if the gun works! This
particular morning I rose at five o'clock, thinking that all
hunters had to be up and around before the animals were. I
donned blue jeans, woolen shirt and high boots, and was just
stepping quietly outside when Curly awoke. "Where are you
going?" he asked.

"Hunting."

"Something will get you."

"No, it won't—what do you mean!"

"OK," he laughed. "Go on, you'll learn better some day."

I stepped outside and closed the door behind me. It was
dark, and the air was clammy and cold. My enthusiasm left me
and I wished I were back in my warm bed with the blanket
pulled up under my chin. Something will get me, huh!

Something will get me indeed. Wouldn't Curly be surprised if I came home with four birds.

I climbed the ridge back of the camp, gingerly stepping along with the twenty-two rifle over my shoulder. It was gloomy, and after I had walked about three hundred yards, I suddenly recalled the bear and bobcat stories I had heard. That was too much, and I looked around for a big tree to sit under, lean against and think it over.

Calming down a bit and pooh-poohing all those silly wild tales, a sudden hoot from an owl not far from me brought me to my feet. The gun was forgotten and my heart fluttered wildly. I'd have run if I could, but I was frozen in my tracks. When I recognized the weird sound, I laughed aloud, and for a minute the idiotic noise echoed around me. I foolishly sat down again, listening to the tiny, rustling noises of little forest animals and fighting back a desire to go home.

When I did get back to camp, Curly was frying bacon and eggs. "Where's your birds?" he asked.

"The last I saw of them they were heading for the border. I was walking up the road, when Wango! One banged me in the face, and three more were right behind it. I was walking down the road when Wheee! Six more flew up, and when I was almost to camp—there was the biggest deer in the middle of the road, and he had the biggest set of antlers I ever saw—"

"Why didn't you shoot them?" Curly interrupted.

I listlessly sat down on the couch. My knees were shaky and I dropped the gun I had been holding. Curly turned around and looked at me. "Oho! Buck fever! I'll be damned. Better go to bed and sleep it off."

I went to bed, and I must have "slept it off" because I've shot many partridges since then.

I missed more partridges than I hit, but after a season's practice I could pick up a limit of four in a flock. (I like to brag, now that I have an excuse for it.) We used the twenty-two rifle because we didn't like to bite into bird shot, and we had very few "tower" on us. A bird will tower if it isn't killed outright. It flies straight up into the air with head pointed to the sky and wings beating furiously and loudly, and when it is thirty or forty feet up, it levels off and falls. The bird is dead when it reaches the peak of its tower.

The Indians call the partridge *Mitchiwess*—"the canoe builder for all the animals." His drumming in the woods sounded like an Indian building his birch-bark canoe. Mitchiwess resolved to build a marvel canoe. If a canoe had two ends and could go two ways, why not a round canoe that could go all ways?

Mitchiwess called forth all the tribes—the bear, the wood-chuck, the owl, the blue jay and the porcupine—to watch the first performance of the wonderful round canoe. When Mitchiwess got into the canoe and paddled, all he did was go round and round. He was so chagrined and shamed that he went back into the deep woods to stay, and that is why the partridge is an inland bird.

I have never been able to locate a partridge when it was drumming, and I know few people who have. It has been done. Photographs and movies have been taken of a partridge when it was drumming. It is not the beating of wings against a hollow log that makes the drumming noise, but an upward and outward beating of wings against the air. Once a partridge starts drumming, it can't stop, no matter how close danger may be. I have heard it described as a shiver, with feathers ruffed and the bird seeming as big as a turkey.

They do not drum only in the springtime. I have heard them in the middle of winter, late fall and midsummer, both

Photo courtesy of Helen Lennon
Helen Hamlin and two of her dogs standing outside the two-room warden's cabin at Umsaskis Lake.

night and day. The noise is hard to locate and when it is close it seems to come from all directions.

October in the north woods is breathtakingly beautiful. The days are warm, lazy and calm. The lakes are mirrors reflecting the deep blue of the skies and the gaudily colored, panoramic shores—golden beeches, crimson maples, bright-yellow birches, wine-colored ash, a background of dark spruces and firs and lavender distances. The season is short—as short as a north woods spring—and Nature indulges in all her capricious fancies to make it a brilliant one.

One morning we wakened to a darkened day to hear the wind howling through the forest, gustily sweeping rain and leaves before it, and whipping the lake water to white-capped waves. After the three-day storm, all is drab and colorless. The cold weather is no longer confined to the nights, and the skies are heavy with snow-laden clouds.

There were few people in the country. Three families lived at Churchill. The Bridges and Cyril Jandreau were at Umsaskis, but they planned to move away before the road closed. Four people lived at Clayton Lake. Another game warden and his wife were at Nine Mile, but they planned to spend the winter in Lac Frontiere. Three bachelor trappers had headquarters in an old lumber camp at the St. John River, and Jim Gardner was at Long Lake dam as caretaker through the winter. We were a handful of people in four thousand square miles of woods, with forty-three miles of road that would be closed during the winter.

The Maine Forestry Service has a network of telephone lines through the country, down the Allagash and St. John rivers, through the Musquacook lakes, Eagle Lake, and down to Chesuncook Village, with switches in the more frequently used camps to shift calls and relay them. They were our only connection with the outside world, a slender thread through miles of forests, and it was sometimes broken by falling trees or carried away on the antlers of a moose.

Cyril Jandreau lived in the fire warden's camp below us. He trapped that fall and fleshed his mink and otter pelts by the light from our gasoline lantern. Cyril has an encyclopedic knowledge of the ways of the woods, and he never tired of answering my foolish questions. The first time I saw him I thought he was the homeliest man I had ever seen. The next time I saw him I thought he was nice. Now I think there is no one quite like Cyril Jandreau. He is a lumberman, guide, "river hog," woodsman, trapper, fire warden and the best company in the world. It is difficult to describe Cyril. He is Allagash—Lincolnesque—and has a physical fitness that belies his fifty years. He has a broad forehead, widely spaced brown eyes, a heavy nose, full lips and a slightly bald head. He is as tall as Curly, has a barrel chest, a once slender waistline that is now giving way to middle age, and the long clean-cut legs of a woodsman. What impresses me most about Cyril is his quiet reserve, a low deep-throated laugh, and the curious expression on his face. He looks hard, and yet he has that puzzled look about his eyes that I have seen on very few men—men who are exceptionally keen and have had no schooling whatever. Cyril is sensitive about his inability to read and write, and the first time he wanted me to read some letters for him and answer them, Curly had to be the go-between. I had to be asked, my answer given, the time arranged, and finally Cyril appeared at the camp with the letters and writing paper. During his career as jobber and woods boss, Cyril kept all records of the operation in a mental notebook.

The Bridges are also incomparable. They are as ageless and modern as the woods they have lived in for so long. If things became dull at our camp, I would walk the half mile to call on the Bridges.

Mrs. Bridges, a bundle of vitality, would be bouncing from room to room, with all doors and windows open in the camp. "Come in quick and help me!" She was breathless. "These pesky flies are driving me crazy! Shoo! Shoo! God's sake!" Waving a towel she chased a few more through the doorway. "Drive them out of the bedroom and start closing the windows. What have you been doing? Where is Curly? I hoped he would be over. God's sake! I have half a rhubarb pie we can't eat, and I thought he would get rid of it for me. That man is the best garbage pail I ever saw!"

I never had time to answer her questions. She continued: "I've got the darndest crick in my back. Are you going to the dance at Lac Frontiere tonight? There's the telephone again. God's sake! Hello?"

An endless conversation followed.

Bridgie strolled in. "Hi, have a cigarette. Curly with you? Tell him I've fixed that motor."

Mrs. Bridges was through at the telephone. "Helen Hamlin! Get your big feet off my clean couch cover. Are you going to the dance? Ouch! My back feels like a ramrod. I haven't been able to do a thing today. God's sake! By the time I got my washing on the line I only had time to put up twenty quarts of pickles."

"Br-r-r-r," the telephone interrupted. Bridgie winked and I put my feet back on the couch.

In November, thousands of white fish choke and boil through a narrow waterway at Chamberlain Lock dam on their way to spawning beds. Joe Giguare had a permit to net them to use for bait in his traps and he gave us a bushel of white fish. Curly smoked them. He built a fish-smoking contraption—a barrel with no top and no bottom, and laced through with wires to lay the fish on. He split the fish, cleaned and wiped them dry, and over a bed of hot, glowing coals in the outdoor fireplace, he spread a generous layer of green maple chips. He placed the open barrel over it, laid the fish on the wires and covered the top with a burlap bag to keep the smoke in.

All day he watched and tasted, tore in and out of the camp, let in the flies and made a general nuisance of himself.

"Taste this one! Just taste it!"

"I can't. I've eaten four already."

"But taste this one! This is good!" He stuck it under my nose.

"Now you get out of here! I'm all done tasting. The last one I ate was raw."

When they were done, tawny colored and crisp, we packed them in a box between layers of waxed paper and put them in the springhouse. Temptation was too strong when I went out for a pail of water; one tasted like more, until I felt like the cat that licked the cream. I had no trouble getting Curly to carry water on washday. While they lasted—Monday was smoked-fish day.

Chapter 12
A Warden's Work

Curly's work called him everywhere. He traveled by car when he could, or by canoe, but mostly he covered his territory on foot. He checked hunters, fishermen and trap lines for licenses and a legal share of nature's bounty. The French call a game warden a *garde de chasse*—keeper of hunting—completely descriptive and explanatory.

To some people (fish hogs, beaver poachers and night hunters), a game warden is the lowest form of humanity. Others regard him as the Maine version of the romantic Mounted Police of Curwood's novels. Warden work is neither sneaky nor easy. It is just a job like any other kind of job. A game warden's special abilities include a primitive knowledge of how to live in the woods, something very few people acquire.

Ask a warden what he thinks about his work and he will growl and gripe about the long hours, the low wages and the many sleepless nights spent in the open on a smelt brook or in a deer yard. Ask him if he would rather do something else and he starts to hedge. He likes his work and wouldn't change places with "Rockerfeller."

How does a game warden catch a poacher? That is a question I have often been asked. I don't know. I have heard game wardens talk shop when they get together and they sound like comic-strip Supermen. Each story outrivals the last one. The only thing I learned is that they are master storytellers.

In northern Aroostook the work is somewhat different than it is in the southern part of the state. The country is sparsely populated and the game warden has to depend on primitive means of transportation to ferret out his information on night hunting and illegal trapping. Curly did this by poling and using an outboard motor over many miles of water by canoe, and walking many more miles through uncharted wilderness. If fishing parties came through the Allagash headwaters from Moosehead Lake, he had to drive to Churchill by car, and to Eagle Lake and Chamberlain Lake by canoe. If night hunters were on the Maine-Canadian boundary he had to spend most of his nights out there, rolled up in a sleeping bag to keep warm. If he was patrolling some forest tract and discovered an unknown and unmarked trap line, he had to follow it to the trapper's headquarters.

There are no exacting working hours for a game warden and no special procedure for going about his duties. One time Curly was coming home through Long Lake and he noticed a camp site on the lake. He stopped to investigate, observed that there had been efforts to conceal the fact that someone had slept there overnight, and he became curious. There had been no fishing parties through the country for the past two weeks. It could be someone who came up the river only as far as here, but why Long Lake? Umsaskis with its better camping spots for sportsmen was only a few miles distant. He walked around and discovered footprints. There was no mark on the shore to show where a canoe had rested, so the person must have been on foot. Who was he and what was he doing? Back of the screening growth of new spruces around the camp site were the distinct traces of an old tote road. This was the way the night visitor had come. He searched the banks of the small brook that ran into the lake, and a hundred yards from the mouth he discovered a mink set—a trap baited with fish and set underwater for mink. He picked up the trap to inspect it and found that there was no name on it. Whoever was trapping here was doing it illegally.

It was getting dark so Curly came back to camp. I packed his knapsack that night and the next morning he rose at four o'clock, had his breakfast and left for Long Lake by canoe. At the camp site he pulled his canoe up on the shore, turned it over and put the motor under it. Then he started up the old tote road that followed the brook, carrying his knapsack with beans, bacon, biscuits and a tea pail, an ax in his hands, and an automatic in a shoulder holster. A mile farther on he discovered two more mink sets, also without name or address.

By noon he had left the brook, and at dusk he reached the St. John River, traveling directly northwest. He found no more signs of the poacher, but on the bank of the St. John was another mink set. By now he had decided that the fellow must be a Canadian and that there was little hope of catching him. Should he go back or go on? It looked as though he were going to stay there that night. He could walk up the river seven miles to the camps at Nine Mile on the La Croix road, or he could walk down the river two miles to the farms at Seven Islands and stay there overnight. Perhaps it would be wiser not to be seen at Seven Islands. He built his campfire back from the shore behind a fallen log and ate the last of his lunch. Tomorrow he could shoot a few partridges and eat them. The early-fall air was cold, and that night it snowed—not much, just a spit of snow, but cold. Curly didn't sleep much because he had to keep his fire going, and when dawn came he had a drink of water from the river and shouldered his empty knapsack.

Walking up the bank he discovered a place to wade across. On the other shore he followed up the small brook that ran into the St. John and found a new beaver house and dam, with four traps at the entrance to the beaver house.

The woods here were thick, and he traveled by compass. For miles he walked over blowdown—a tangled mass of fallen timbers lying crisscross as they had fallen during a hurricane. For hours he never set his foot on the ground, and at times he found himself fifteen feet in the air, floundering through a maze of fallen trees. Once out of the blowdown, he was traveling through a marsh. He shot two partridges and stopped to build a fire to cook them. That afternoon he reached Big Black River, just two miles below its outlet at Depot Lake, and he walked up to the old camp there, one that might have been used as a headquarters. The camp was empty but had obviously been used, for there were signs of recent occupancy. What should he do? The trapper, he had decided, was definitely a Canadian. He probably wouldn't be in to tend his traps for a week yet. There was one chance in a thousand of catching him, and it was too small a chance in that enormous tract of woodland. He started for home, walking around Depot Lake and picking up a tote road that led out to the main road. Bridgie gave him a ride to Umsaskis. The next day Cyril took him down to Long Lake to get his canoe. What had he accomplished? Probably nothing. He had picked up the traps and thrown them away. He had left a warden card at the Depot camp, merely as a warning. How far had he walked? Probably thirty miles as the crow flies. Two days later he drove to St.

Adelbert on the Canadian boundary, stopped at the small general
store and questioned the storekeeper, merely to start a rumor.
Then he drove along the range roads close to the boundary and
wherever he saw a house he stopped the car, got out and searched
the woods toward the boundary. A week later he visited the
Depot camp and found everything as he had left it.

It seems like a roundabout way of doing game-warden work,
but that's the way it has to be in the type of country he was in.
In all the four years he spent in the Allagash wilderness he had
only two prosecutions for fish and game violations, whereas
down-country in one year he had over thirty. One of the violations up-country was illegal possession of too many fish by a
young couple who just couldn't believe that there were that
many trout. Even if they couldn't keep all their trout to take
back to show their friends, they gladly paid their fine in Dover-
Foxcroft and sent us a Christmas present that year!

The people who lived in that country were not poachers.
They had as much respect for game conservation as the warden
did. Undoubtedly range-road Canadians made excursions on our
side of the boundary, as some of the young men from Lac
Frontiere later admitted to Curly. The young people in that border town had a sort of recreation hall sponsored by the Canadian
government; Curly donated a set of boxing gloves and often
spent an afternoon with them at their hall. They actually told
him he was a good fellow for an American, and they wouldn't
trap in his district anymore!

There were a few fall hunters whose reputations had preceded
them, and who had to be watched. One party particularly had
an annoying habit of telephoning our camp at night to find out if
the game warden was home. They called themselves sportsmen. It

was too obvious, and Curly spent all the nights they were in the country lying out watching their camp.

I often wondered why it was when Curly was stopping cars and searching them that he went over some cars diligently and others he let pass with only a cursory examination. He says he knows the minute he opens the car door. He has done it so often, experience has probably taught him who looks guilty and who doesn't. An extra hindquarter of deer has often been hidden in another deer carcass, and fish have been hidden in toolboxes and under seat cushions. During hunting season he stops a car, opens the door, watches the hands of the occupants to see that they don't hide anything, and quickly and smoothly picks up their guns and breaks them open to see if they are loaded. It isn't because of game conservation that it is illegal to have a loaded gun in a car but because of personal safety to the sportsman.

A woman who tags a deer immediately falls under suspicion. A surprising number of women actually do shoot their deer, but most of them don't. A game warden (I won't mention names) once questioned a woman's statement that she did shoot her deer.

"If you could shoot that deer at the range you said you did," the warden argued, "let's see you hit this watch." He pulled an heirloom out of his pocket and backed off a hundred yards. The lady shattered it with one shot, leaving the warden with his jaw hanging open.

The lady's husband, too late, volunteered the information that his wife was a "shootin' fool." She gave exhibitions for an ammunition corporation.

One part of Curly's work that I liked best were the long three- and four-day canoe trips that we took during the summertime, trips where he made a sort of inspection tour up and down the rivers and through the chain of lakes. We camped away from home, staying in deserted cabins and outlying warden camps. During the wintertime these inspection trips were less frequent because of the difficulty of traveling. He went on snowshoes, and when we had the dogs he used them as a means of transportation. This was routine work.

If anyone is lost, the game warden is called to find him. If anyone is drowned the game warden is called to drag the lake. If dogs are killing deer (as they do on a crust in March) the warden is called. If a moose (usually a sick one) is hanging around a camp, the warden is called either to drive him away or drag him away. If some trapper hasn't been heard from in the wintertime, the game warden visits him, mostly to see if he is alive. If the cabin is occupied by a corpse, again the game warden has to notify the proper authorities and help drag the body out to civilization. This happened once to Curly. Tragedy has to be taken matter-of-factly in the woods.

Two old trappers who were living quite far back hadn't been heard of for some time, and one February day Curly called at their camp. He found them hale and hearty. They were making home-brew. One old duffer was sitting on one side of the keg and the other was sitting opposite him. It was apparent that they hadn't been able to wait until the beer was ready before sampling it. On top of the keg was a little knothole, with two nails bent over it, holding a little paper windmill that spun merrily in the escaping gas.

Curly's district included 22 townships—792 square miles of woods, 31 recorded lakes and ponds, a number of unnamed ponds, and probably some unknown ones, since the country has never been completely surveyed. It's a lot of country, but it is merely a fraction of the entire wilderness.

A Canadian patrol plane crashed on East Lake, the most desolate and impossible spot to reach on the whole boundary wilderness. Two men out of seven survived, and they had wandered as far as the small lumber camp on Two Mile Brook, north of St. Pamphile.

Many Allagash woodsmen and a few game wardens were called upon to lead search and rescue parties into East Lake. One of the scouts was David Jackson, game warden for the inland Fish and Game Department. He knows that country as well as he does the palm of his hand. He has cruised the woods all his life, and he is the best canoeman in the state of Maine. My hat goes off to Dave when I hear the often-repeated tales of his running Devil's Elbow on a spring freshet, or how he bluffed two backwoods Canadian poachers into disarming when they had the drop on him and were holding him off with a rifle. That is one story I had to pry out of Dave with a lot of questions.

"Where did this happen, Dave?" I asked.

He was quiet a while. "Over in East Lake country," he finally said.

"But how did you know they were there?" I asked.

Dave speaks very slowly, seeming to choose his words. "Followed their trap line and jumped 'em—the gol darned fools."

"I thought they had a gun, Dave," I said.

He was silent for a long time. "Did," he said. "Twenty-two. Told 'em to lay it down." Dave looked at me and I could understand why the two outlaws finally came out from behind their sheltering tree and passed over the gun. Dave's eyes are steely. He looks like an Indian, except that his features are finely drawn. He is a slight, wiry person.

Dave once had tremendous stamina and endurance, but too many long, weary woods miles on an empty stomach have finally injured his health. Even today, no one can run Big Black Rapids as easily as Dave can at all heights of water, and no one can travel in the woods as quickly and easily as he can, with only matches and a sheath knife.

Chapter 13

Digging In

S uch a way of life did not seem unusual to us. We liked it, and started to dig in for the winter. We bought our winter groceries at Sanders' store in Greenville, Maine—a four-hundred-mile round trip through Canada and back into the States again.

If there is anything in the world you want, you can probably buy it at Sanders'. If you want to know where you are, where you're going and what you need, you can find out at Sanders'. It is a small-town general store and at the same time a headquarters for sportsmen. You can buy S. S. Pierce canned goods, or a less luxurious brand. You can buy fishing tackle of all descriptions and varieties, choice steaks, outboard motors, camp kits, ladies' lingerie, excellent outdoor clothing, expensive toiletries, yard goods, hardware, fresh vegetables, dishes, children's toys, magazines, salt pork, potatoes, and any kind of outdoor boot, shoe or moccasin. You can even borrow a few dollars. All this is flavored with a salty, running commentary by either of the Sanders brothers, Harry and Paul. You are greeted like a long-lost brother, and they watch for you when spring comes. A sportsman once doubted Sanders' reputation for producing anything and everything from this out-of-the-way store. "If you have a pulpit," he said, "I'll buy it." The pulpit was found in the back of the store-house. I wanted one of those old-fashioned butter dishes with a rounded cover on it, and Nick, one of the clerks, found one in the basement covered with layers and layers of the years' accumulation of dust.

We made two trips downriver, the last visits until next spring. Never having bought a six months' supply of groceries ahead of time, neither of us knew exactly what we would need, but we listed what we thought two people would eat, forgetting many things and miscalculating on others. Among our items were flour, sugar, salt, spices, vanilla, cereals, cornmeal, cheese, baking powder, soda, dry yeast, lard, cocoa, coffee, tea, canned milk, canned vegetables, fruits, fish, meat, dried apples, apricots, prunes, crackers, spaghetti, onions, potatoes, ham, molasses, pork, bologna, bacon, soap, butter, matches, desserts and tobacco.

By the time we reached tobacco, the list was long and the purse was thin, and we bought the "makings"—loose tobacco and those aggravating zigzag cigarette papers that take a handful of matches to keep a cigarette burning. We rolled our own. It takes practice, and my first ones were like wrapped molasses kisses with both ends twisted. After a winter's practice I could roll a decent cigarette. Curly rolled "knitting needles" that flared at the touch of a match, while my "cigars" lasted half an hour, and I had to keep spitting out the excess tobacco that stuck to my tongue.

Much to Curly's disgust, I always forgot to put the cover back on the tobacco can, and upon arising one morning, I found him diligently stirring an evil-smelling concoction over the fire. I thought he had been rather quiet, not the usual hurry-up-and-get-up-I-want-my-breakfast morning.

"What in the world are you doing?" I got a whiff of it. "What is it?"

"Tobacco."

"Lady Nicotine never looked like that. What did you do to it?"

"It's your fault. You left the cover off and it dried up."

"But what did you do to it?" I asked.

"I put water in it."

"Water! What are you cooking it for?"

"To boil the water off, of course. I put in just a little bit too much."

We stored our groceries in the bedroom, the springhouse, and in the hole under the floor that served as a cellar, further decorating it with mousetraps. It seemed like a lot of food for two people, and we thought we would never eat it all.

We were almost ready for winter, but we couldn't sit around and "let 'er snow" until we'd gone deer hunting. Deer meat is a necessity in that country because fresh meat is not available on our side of the boundary.

The weather is still warm when the deer season opens. When the nights grow cold and the mornings frosty, the deer will be seen running across the road and wary of any sign of danger. The coldest mornings, or after the first snowstorm, are the best for deer hunting, for then the deer are bewildered by the strange snow; they will be moving from their lairs in swamps and valleys to roam the ridges for the warming sunshine and to search for fallen beechnuts.

One afternoon I stood for twenty minutes watching three deer on a ridge. They seemed to be watching me as they stood with heads lowered and motionless, their noses pointed toward me; their eyesight is not well developed and they were trying to locate the noise I had made when walking through the fallen leaves. The wind was toward me and I cautiously advanced until they were but twenty feet away. The buck wheeled and sprang into the bushes, followed by the two does, all with flags waving—the white underside of a deer's short tail—and the last part to be seen as they gracefully leap into the woods. It was then I remembered that I had a loaded thirty-two special rifle in my hand.

I have only once in my life seen a deer stumble as it sailed over a tangled mass of fallen trees. The deer landed and dropped to its knees, but never stopped. It bounded up and was off again. Deer, standing still, to my way of thinking, are not beautiful creatures. They are graceful when running and jumping, but their large bodies are out of proportion to their thin legs and small, narrow heads. Their ears are mulish. They even walk awkwardly.

I suppose I should feel squeamish about shooting deer or partridge. I like the animals in the woods. I have lived among them and I know their habits fairly well. I do not kill for glory or excitement. The best part of hunting to me is the excuse to be outdoors, but it is a case of "no shootee, no eatee." I did my share and shot my deer.

I prefer to hunt alone. Curly was a bit skeptical about my chances of finding my way home and insisted that I carry a compass. I never used it because I never was lost, and I never was lost because I never traveled very far. I poke along, walk for hours and only cover a few miles.

One of the first times Curly took me on a woods hike with him, we walked from Churchill Lake to Spider Lake—ten endless woods miles across country and partly following a telephone line. I had discarded my blue jeans and moccasins for a pair of fancy, gracefully flared knee-tight breeches and a pair of high, laced, shiny leather boots.

We came to Pleasant Stream and Curly waded across. I looked at my new boots and hesitated. "Aren't you going to carry me?"

"What! Well, I guess not. Come on, don't be a sissy."

"These boots cost me six bucks, but if you feel so extravagant, OK." I waded across and discovered that my boots leaked. They usually do leak when water goes over the tops.

Curly set the pace, and I steamed up the ridges behind him, grunted through swamps, stopped and looked around when he did, and saw nothing until he pointed to the partridge that was three feet from me. I had been gazing into the distance, expecting to see a dinosaur.

Apparently this was to be a silent affair with all conversation eschewed. We walked and walked. My breeches were too tight. I was plastered with mud from wading through black, mucky swamps. My shirt collar was filled with twigs, dead leaves and scratchy beechnuts. My face was lacerated because on one occasion I hadn't ducked quickly enough. We went up a ridge and down a ridge, through a mudhole and up another ridge.

We came to a big mudhole this time.

"Do we wade through this?" I stopped, glad of a chance to get my breath.

"Wade through it? This is Spider Lake!"

"Do we eat now?"

"Better eat on the way back. It's getting dark early."

We turned and walked back. I was getting madder every minute and the blister on my heel didn't help any.

"Why didn't we see any deer?" I was still able to forgive and forget.

"Deer? Hell no! You made so much noise you scared them all out of the country. I just wanted to see if it was moose country."

Merciful heavens! My new boots ruined for that!

We shot our deer in the late fall, skinned and quartered them, and hung them on the shed rafters to freeze and keep. The meat formed a dry, leathery, protective coating on the outside, and as we needed it, a hindquarter or a saddle was brought into the camp and allowed to thaw slowly. When the outside was trimmed off, we had steak that was so tender it could be cut with a fork.

The weather was freezing cold and it wasn't long before the lake was frozen. In December, snow came to stay. We had had several flurries and sometimes three or four inches of snow in a single storm, but it always melted. This time the quiet, giant flakes were at first absorbed by the earth, but as the cold grew sharper, they gradually covered the frozen ground and clung to the evergreens.

While the road was still open we made several trips to Lac Frontiere for "fresh" eggs. The grocer said they were fresh because they came from "hon top of Quebec," but they must have been there when the city walls were built. We had to throw half of them away.

At New Year's we attended the birthday party at Druins' and had a real French Canadian supper. I like the French Canadian dishes. I never can remember the name of my favorite dish, but I think it is called *croteau*, a meat pie made with two pastry crusts and filled with a spiced ground pork. Everyone knows what hogshead cheese is—*fromage de tête de cochon*—and then there is *boudain*.

It was Curly's first introduction to *boudain*, a dark, rich sausage. "What is it?" he asked.

"Try it, it's good." I passed him the platter.

"It *is* good. Melts in your mouth. Never tasted anything like it. But what is it?"

"Pig's blood, curdled and spiced."

"HUH! I mean, all right—well, anyway, pass me the *boudain*. It's damn good."

Every snowstorm brought anywhere from four to fourteen inches of snow, and the road was soon closed. We had been expecting it for so long that it was in a sense a relief when we were shut in. Everything we wanted was at camp, and there were a few of the books and magazines we had brought in on our last trip downriver that hadn't been read yet. There were twenty-nine people left in the country, counting Joe Giguare's eight children. We were alone at Umsaskis with Boots, a lady dog—who looked like a cross between a sawhorse and a cant dog, and good company when she wasn't a nuisance. She nearly went crazy sniffing the countless rabbit tracks in the dooryard.

At first we didn't mind being confined to the small camp. It was warm and cozy, and after the hectic running around and trying to squeeze everything into what little time was left before the road closed, it was nice to be quiet and sleep and rest.

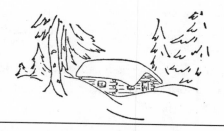

Chapter 14

Snowbound

We were actually snowbound. Cyril Jandreau and the Bridges had moved out of the country before January and we were in sole possession of Umsaskis for the winter. Our nearest neighbors were ten miles away and the nearest town was fifty miles away directly across country through the woods. We had only ourselves to depend on, and in the gradual settling for winter we began to look forward to small events, most particularly to mail.

We had but little mail that winter. A company tractor made one trip to Lac Frontiere before the snow became too deep and they brought the mail as far as Churchill. The mailman snowshoed to Clayton with two dogs and a sled to bring in the mail, but that was less than a trip a month, and it only came as far as Clayton Lake. Curly harnessed Boots to the single sled and went for our mail. It was a one-day trip, but even eighteen miles on snowshoes is tiring.

Mail day was a holiday. There was a collection of newspapers and letters to read, and on rare occasions there were packages to be opened. When I could send mail, I sent advertising coupons that I cut from magazines for toothpaste, shaving cream, chocolate milk powders, hand lotion, cosmetics and recipe pamphlets. Some of them required a dime with the coupon, but it was worth it just to get a package in the mail.

Curly was as interested in them as I was. "Gee, look at all the packages. Here's some shaving cream. I hope it isn't that brushless stuff. What's that?"

"Cosmetics."

"Cost who?" he growled.

"Powder, rouge and lipstick."

"But it says for redheads, and here's some for brunettes. You can't put on that stuff."

"Whoa, now, wait a minute. Don't you put that on the dog. You used my last bottle of perfume on her the other day."

We had ordered some things from a mail-order catalogue, including small parts for the car that Curly entertained himself by tinkering with. Six weeks later the postmaster called on the phone and said we had a package at Clayton. Curly went for our mail and came back hopping mad. "Of all the bald-headed outfits!" he sputtered. "Eighteen miles for this!"

"What is it?"

He looked at me suspiciously. "Did you order this?" He threw six powder puffs on the table.

"No, I didn't order it."

"Well, that's supposed to be spark plugs. If I ever lay my hands on the pinhead that sent them I'll tie him in a knot!"

Boots hated to be harnessed to go to Clayton. She was perfectly capable of hauling a small load, but like all house pets, she was lazy. She had a sneaky disposition at times, a gluttonous appetite all the time, and she stole everything she could find— but she was my dog and I liked her. Curly couldn't do anything with her, and when she was harnessed to the sled she would get ahead of him on the trail and hightail it for home—pure cussedness and a desire to sleep behind the stove.

The first time she ran away from him, she was hauling a can of gasoline to the main road. Curly let her go ahead, and that was the last we saw of Boots until late that night. The can of gasoline upset on the first curve, and Boots's tracks were headed toward Churchill, eleven miles away.

Late that afternoon Anna called me on the telephone. "Your dog is here."

"Is she still harnessed to the sled?"

"Yes. What will we do with her?"

"Turn her around and head her for home."

When Boots bumped onto the porch again, she was covered with white frost and really had an excuse for lying behind the stove and groaning all night.

What little housework there was to do was not enough to keep me busy, and the less I had to do, the less I wanted to do. At first I spent quite a bit of time and imagination on meals; then, when I had exhausted our variety of foods, I wasn't so particular about insisting on hot biscuits with our supper. When I mopped the linoleum, Curly usually tore into the camp with two more pails of water. His frozen moccasins skidded on the wet floor, and he would land in a heap with the water fast spreading around him.

"Jeepers! That water is cold!"

"Tanglefoot! Now I'll have to mop this again."

"You won't get it mopped if you don't close the door. I'll freeze here."

Once in a while he managed to keep one pail upright, with the other rakishly perched on his head.

I hated washday. We had one tub, a washboard and no wringer. Water was heated in the tub, the clothes were scrubbed and wrung by hand, and another tub of water was heated to boil the towels and sheets. When that was done, another tub of water was heated to rinse them. It was suppertime before I had the clothes hung on the line, and it would be so cold outside I could only hang one piece at a time before I had to run back into the camp to warm my hands. Curly's union suits were so long I had to hang them to the branch of a tree, and they would greet us, gently and stiffly waving in the breeze, when we opened the door.

My troubles weren't over then. Another tub of water was heated to wash Curly. He gingerly stuck his big toe in the water and backed off, horrified.

"It's cold! Why can't I wait until spring?"

"No, it isn't cold. Now get in."

"It's hot then!" he howled.

"Stop your fussing and get in. Here's your soap and be sure you use it!"

"That whole cake? I'll be here all night. Here, Boots, have some soap. Put the dog in too and we'll all smell like violets."

We ate and ate, and with no hard work to do, it seemed likely that we would get fat. But being alone will make anyone skinny. The trapper, cruiser or any other woodsman is not fat, and it isn't entirely due to hard work and scanty meals. Too much desolation will change the pounds to ounces, and the work they do will make every bit of flesh as sinewy, wiry and tough as leather.

We didn't have any diversions. For a while I sewed and made over a few of my clothes. When I had to fix a hem, I had Curly try on the dress and stand on the table.

"Hurry up," he sputtered. "Someone will come in and catch me in this."

"If you don't stop wiggling I'll never get it done. And if there is anyone around here that is apt to pop in, I'd like to see them."

"Ouch! I'm not a pincushion. Where'd you get the fancy buttons? Why don't you put some like that on my shirts?"

We had long since read all the books and magazines that we thought would last all winter. We played cribbage until the sight of a cribbage board was sickening—fifteen two, fifteen four and a pair is six, and nine times out of ten I was trimmed. Where Curly got all those twenty-four hands, I'm sure I don't know. If I cut a jack, I figured I was lucky to get a free peg.

Curly knew how to play chess. We had a checkerboard and we looked in a mail-order catalogue to see what the chessmen were like. I cut bishops, knights, and castles from cardboard,

A cluster of sporting camps at Umsaskis Lake.

and Curly sawed little square blocks of wood to paste onto them as a base. We painted one set red and the other yellow.

He taught me how to play by checking me in three moves, but it was the other way around before the winter was over. Some of the games lasted for hours with much arguing on both sides.

"You're checked," I declared triumphantly.

"No, I'm not. I can get out here."

"You can't. Where's my bishop? You took my bishop! You weren't supposed to take that. Give me my bishop! I'll wallop you with a pillow. I want my bishop!"

The game ended on a snowbank outside with Boots delightedly prancing and kicking up more snow and feathers, and with us minus another pillow.

I played solitaire until the cards were so thin and ragged that washing and ironing them wouldn't bring back the king's whiskers. I kept my score and made "eighty dollars" while the cards lasted.

I resorted to the crossword puzzles from the collection of newspapers that were in the shed, even from the cupboard shelves and the bottom of trunks. When those were gone I made my own crossword puzzles, and if I wasn't woods queer by then, I should have been.

Curly's particular pastime was lying on the couch with the twenty-two rifle perched on his knees, shooting the mice and houseflies on the rafters. I will say he was good at it. I don't know if he hit the flies, because all that was left for evidence was a hole, but I'll take his word for it.

I will confess that we spent a lot of our time listening in on the telephone, and sometimes joining the conversation. Everyone else in the country did the same thing, and as many as six would be talking at once, in both French and English. Curly and Jim

Gardner were the only two in the country who couldn't speak French, and Mrs. Deblois and Mr. Druin were the only ones who couldn't speak English. If matters of great importance arose, such as the mail coming to Clayton, or an airplane seen overhead, the telephone rang like mad. When Curly answered our ring, it was usually—"Hello. *Une* min-u-tee *la*! Come quick, Pooie! It's talking French!"

That's the way it was once when I was kneading bread with my hands all doughy and trying to think of a six-letter word for the albumose in seralbumin. The conversation was a recipe for cream pie or date squares, a discussion about the weather and an early spring predicted, or a request to ring Long Lake dam, so Long Lake dam could ring Dickey Central, so Dickey Central could relay a call somewhere in civilization.

Everyone has heard of the Frenchman who had a telephone installed in his home and insisted on one that talked French. The same story is told about a radio.

Then there was the time I answered the phone when someone from along the Allagash called.

" 'ello, Curlee? Dat you?"

"No, this is Mrs. Curly."

"Oh, Madame Curlee. Dat you?"

"Yes, this is me."

"I jess ring to see hif de moose she's brak de line."

"No, the line isn't broken."

"Wall, dat moose she's brak him somewares, but I tink me she's not brak too far part, cause I 'ear you leetle bit."

Our only hope was that the line wouldn't be broken, and we called Dickey Central after every storm to see if it was still intact. A heavy snowstorm that coated the trees and wires made it almost impossible to call downriver.

Curly once had an old radio that he hooked to the telephone line for an aerial, and on shortwave stations a telephone conversation could be heard clearly. We received quite a surprise one day when we heard the postmistress's voice coming over the radio. "I have a letter here for you, but you owe me three cents on it."

Curly's work called him away for several days or a week at a time. He traveled on snowshoes, carrying his food, woolen socks and a blanket in a pack basket strapped to his back, and sleeping in deserted camps wherever the night happened to find him. I didn't mind staying alone. The woods are the safest place in the world. I want to laugh when people say—"Aren't you afraid of bears?" Bears sleep during the winter, and besides, bears are afraid of human beings.

Being alone, and being quiet, is too much. I played the radio as loud as I could and sang for Boots's ungracious benefit. She couldn't drown me out, and she lay behind the stove, groaning and eyeing me mournfully.

Every day I strapped on snowshoes, and Boots and I started for the ridge or across the lake to explore, swinging wide and free in open country or dodging and ducking under heavily laden evergreens. If I stayed in the dooryard and built snow houses, she fell through them. I liked the warm days when the snow was sticky and I made snowmen and -women, and dressed them in clothes and surprised Curly when he came home and found "people" in the yard.

Slowly we grew more aware of our isolation. With each snowstorm we felt less and less delight in its clean white beauty, because it reminded us of the long months to come and of the smallness of our little world at Umsaskis. Despite my love of the woods, I confess that I sometimes found the enforced solitude almost unbearable.

The days were long, and many, many hours I just sat, watching the fire through the open drafts on the hearth, day-dreaming and not interested in much of anything.

Chapter 15
Long, Long Winter

C urly's hair—which gave him his nickname—was quite long by this time, and it hung down over his ears and tickled the back of his neck. We decided it was time he had a haircut.

I opened a barbershop with a pair of shears and a comb, kept cutting until both sides were even, and leveled off with a mixing bowl. It was weird—and so funny. I laughed until I cried just to see the amazed and sorrowful expression on his face when he inspected the work of art with the aid of two mirrors.

"My gosh, woman, what have you done? It will never grow. You gouged it! That's what you were giggling about!"

I had to coax before he let me cut his golden locks again, but we later bought clippers and I can do a good job now. Nothing could be as bad as that first nightmare.

He grew a fire-red, bristling mustache to match the haircut, and he trimmed it much the same way, referring to a movie-magazine picture of Clark Gable. He cut until there was nothing left but a thin line under his nose.

His nose twitched when he snoozed on the couch, and Boots was fascinated by the mustache. She paced back and forth eyeing the nose wiffling, then cautiously approached, thinking it was cookie crumbs. She tried to lap it off. Curly dreamily awoke, gazed into Boots's brown eyes, yelled horribly and bounced over to the sink to shave it off. That was the end of mouse-tashes, and would have been the end of Boots's whiskers if she and I hadn't fled across the lake until he cooled off.

Fudge was a favorite treat that winter, and sometimes we made ice cream. The packaged desserts and canned milk made good ice cream, but I had difficulty preventing Curly from dumping in prunes and coffee grounds.

"Sure, put them in. Didn't you ever hear of coffee ice cream?"

"Yes, but not with coffee grounds. This is supposed to be butterscotch, and you've already added maple syrup and apricots."

"Put in—let's see. What can we put in—here, try this!"

"Now what is it?"

"Blueberries. Canned blueberries!"

He chipped ice from the lake and churned and churned, and when it was hard enough, we sat down on each side of the freezer with the biggest spoons we could find and ate it all. One time we made ice cream with Jell-O, but it was terrible.

When we ran short of tobacco, I saved the cigarette butts, peeled them and steamed the tobacco. Once when Curly was off to Clayton for more tobacco, I steamed the butts from the cigarettes I'd made with the first butts, and by that time a cigarette smelled like a rug burning. He brought back some George Washington pipe tobacco that was all Narciss had left in the company wangan. We ran it through the meat grinder to roll better cigarettes—it took four onions and a loaf of bread to clean the meat grinder.

We began to worry about the radio batteries because they were growing weaker every day. We baked them in the oven for a few minutes of newscast at eight o'clock each evening, but

they didn't last long, and we were in a quandary. They were dry
batteries and we had no way of getting new ones.

From then on we got our "news" over the telephone.
Umsaskis was very quiet now, very cozy. After a day spent outdoors the camp seemed warm and comfortable, and we discarded
our heavy footwear in favor of bedroom slippers. We wore baggy
woolen slacks and shirts anyway, and kept patching them at the
knees and elbows during the winter. We had our supper by
lamplight, lingering over coffee and cigarettes, and when the
dishes were washed and stored away, we reread the few books we
had. Curly read *Black John of Halfaday Creek* by James B.
Hendrix four times that winter, and to this day he talks about
"skulduggery with attempt to hornswoggle." One long winter
day I fussed with my hair, trying to figure out new hairdos.

Sometimes the evenings were desolate with no radio. The
innumerable winter-night noises that we hadn't noticed before
were magnified. We listened to what I have heard described as
quiet. It is not quiet. A frozen twig rasped on the logs of the
camp. Ice buckled on the lake, cracking and rumbling like
thunder as it heaved into ridges when the temperature dropped.
Hoarfrost settled over everything, thickly coating trees and
camp and pit-a-patting on the windowpanes like rain. Lonely
foxes barked on the ridge. The gasoline lantern hissed loudly. A
fire crackled in the stove, and a mouse was in the crackers again.

I sat in the rocking chair with my feet on the hearth, smok-
ing and staring at nothing. Curly lay on the couch with his
hands under his head and stared at the ceiling. Sometimes we
talked, but at times our voices sounded queer. He could always
make me laugh when he'd tell about the club he and a group of
twelve-year-olds in his hometown had organized. It seemed to
consist of initiating someone they didn't like into the club,

making him president if he'd do all the dirty work, and then kicking him out because he was such a blackguard.

Most of the time we talked about the different noises we heard while sitting there, and one wild story would lead to another. I liked to hear an owl hoot—it meant a thaw was coming and the days would be warm. Curly said the most awful thing he ever heard in the woods at night was a Canada lynx—*loupe cervier*, or Indian devil. It sounds like a crazy woman screeching.

We never knew when it was suppertime or bedtime because we didn't keep a clock, and didn't miss one. We could tell time by the radio, but with no radio we didn't know what time it was and we really didn't care. We ate when we were hungry and slept when we were sleepy.

Then our food began to go, for we had made a mistake in estimating our winter's groceries. I had been cooking without eggs, using a cup of snow in cakes, cookies, and muffins and cornstarch in pies and puddings. We shot rabbits for meat, soaked them overnight in soda and water to make them tender, and fried them in hot fat. The first time I fried them this way I forgot to wash off the soda, and we had frothy rabbit for dinner. We had rabbit stews and rabbit pies, but there were many days when we didn't see any rabbits. Our deer meat was gone, and we had one can of roast beef left.

Everything seemed to go at once—vegetables, fruits, cereals, butter, potatoes, cocoa, coffee, tea, peanut butter and milk. With the last of the potatoes and salt pork we had what I call *pommes de terre fricassée*—fried salt pork covered with slices of raw potatoes and water and allowed to simmer until done.

There really wasn't any need for us to run short of food, but since neither of us had ever spent a snowbound winter in the woods before, we just hadn't known how much to buy. The actual quantity of food that two people will eat in six months' time is amazing.

We didn't mind when the coffee was gone. We drank hot water in the mornings. I had no yeast to make bread with, and my experiments with sourdough failed miserably. We ate biscuits. There was no molasses or salt pork for beans, and I cooked them with sugar. We ate rice for cereal until that was gone, and then we started on cornmeal. It was monotonous and flat tasting.

We were hungry, not for just anything to eat but for something new, fresh and buttery tasting. The fancy food advertisements in magazines fascinated us. "Look," Curly held up an advertisement for baking powder containing a picture of a rich, thickly frosted chocolate cake. "How would you like to get on the outside of that?"

"That's nothing. Look at this lobster salad, and all those olives, pickles and deviled eggs. And look at this lemon pie!"

"The more we look at these the hungrier we get."

"I know, but they're hard to resist." I threw mine on the floor and went outside to look at an unchangeable black and white scene, black outlines of trees and the endless white of snowdrifts against the cloudy sky.

Chapter 16

Breaking Trail

It was the first of March and we had to get to Lac Frontiere as best we could. We called Portage Lake via Dickey Central for a plane, and Curly started fixing snowshoes—just in case. We soaked our mukluks in fish oil. Mukluks are untanned sealskin boots that are hand-sewn by Eskimo women. After a great deal of wear they become as soft as gloves, and they are waterproof and warm. They are all made the same size, and when worn for the first time they should be soaked in water and worn while wet. They will shrink or stretch to fit the foot, and seal oil or fish oil will keep them soft.

During the night Curly awoke me. "Boots is eating something and I think it's our mukluks." He turned on the flashlight and we went out. Boots had completely chewed a hole through the heel of one of my mukluks. It was a catastrophe, but Curly patched it with leather, a temporary sewing job that would hold in case I needed them. I always regretted losing those mukluks. They were a Christmas present from Curly, and I was never able to buy another pair like them, with the seal hair still on the outside of the leggings.

We waited and waited for a plane to come, and every day it snowed. We were up at dawn every morning, anxiously watching the gray, overcast sky, hoping to find at least a small patch of blue. But the sky grew darker. The wind was gusty, and by noon it was snowing—fine flakes that came down for hours.

Every high wind over the ridge sounded like a motor, and we would tear outside to listen. It was useless. We went back to the same old meal of beans. For seven hateful days it stormed, and nighttime found us depressed and unwilling to sleep.

One evening, just before dusk, we were sitting in front of the stove toasting our toes on the hearth, grumbling and ill humored, and so sick and tired of cornmush and those nauseatingly pale beans that another meal would have been the final outrage.

"I tell you, Curly, it's useless to wait."

"We've discussed this before, and I won't argue about it now."

"I'm not going to eat any more of those beans. I've snowshoed ten and sixteen miles in a day before I ever heard of a godforsaken hole like Umsaskis."

"This isn't ten or sixteen miles. This is thirty-eight."

"What's the difference? We don't have to do it all in one day. We can stay at Clayton tonight, and at Nine Mile tomorrow night. Let's go. Let's go tonight," I pleaded.

"You win," he grinned. "I don't feel very bean hungry."

I really hustled as I changed to warmer clothing, packed a few clothes in the knapsack and fixed up the camp.

"All ready?" Curly asked.

"Just as soon as I get my parka on. Better call the Druins and tell them we'll be out."

The parkas we had were perfect. There weren't any others like them. A friend of ours had sent us some of that durable, lightweight and windproof Byrd cloth when we hadn't been able to buy it by the yard. I made parkas for both of us, fitting them so they slipped over the head, and the hood fitted snugly without any snaps, elastic or drawstrings. They reached halfway to the knees and had large pockets in front for mittens or anything else we wanted to carry. Curly's was trimmed with a bobcat pelt he had tanned himself, and mine was trimmed with a soft, white fur I had taken from an old pair of lounging pajamas.

We harnessed Boots to the sled, tied on the ax, tea pail and knapsack, and locked the door behind us. It was twilight, lavender and dusky when we strapped on our snowshoes, jumped down off the porch and started along the trail.

As the evening changes to night, the white snow is still visible. The trees had disappeared as though a dark screen, patterned with dull splotches of white snow, were drawn around us. Curly led the way, breaking trail for me, with Boots and the sled behind.

The storm had cleared and the sky twinkled with millions of pinpoints of starlight. It was cold, and it grew colder. The temperature dropped to thirty degrees below zero before we had gone five miles. Only short breaths of air could be sucked through slightly parted lips. Heavy white crystals of frost gathered on Curly's parka and changed him into an icicle man. When he turned around to see how I was coming along, I noticed that his eyebrows and the fur on his hood were white and crystalline. I knew mine were the same. The parka felt heavy and stiff, and I couldn't have raised my eyebrows if I had wanted to. Boots's flanks were covered with frost, and her whiskers were like a bunch of white fluff she was carrying in her mouth. The sled, knapsack, ax and tea pail were white and coated.

Frost is a funny thing. It seems to come down like a light snowfall, but a few feet above, there is nothing. Unlike snow it is hard and cold, and adheres to anything that is warmer than itself. A thin sheet of it over the snow crackles and sputters like a dry cedar log on a fire.

The sharp contraction caused by the sudden drop in temperature would split a tree with a crack like a rifle shot at close range, always startling no matter how many times you've heard it.

We hurried on, running and not stopping to rest. It was torture. I couldn't get a deep breath, but I had to keep my legs swinging, and had to step hard to pound my feet and keep them warm. I beat my mittened hands when we slowed to a fast walk, and Curly urged me into another run.

No one was as glad as I was when we topped Clayton Lake hill and could see the lights at the Druins'—with nine fast miles behind us. We ran down the hill, lifting snowshoes high to keep from stumbling, and dashed across the open settlement. I tried to shout, but couldn't. Boots barked and they heard us coming.

We didn't wait to take off snowshoes but tumbled right inside, and I thought I would suffocate when I felt the warm wave of air from the kitchen. My face was stiff and I couldn't speak.

"*Mais mon Dieu*," Mrs. Druin exclaimed, "you are not frozen?"

"Y-y-yes," I stuttered. "It's c-c-cold tonight."

"*Pauvre chienne*!" Narciss was holding Boots. "Poor dog, this harness is frozen on her."

Curly pulled off his parka. "The darn thing is frozen to my cheeks; they must be frostbitten!"

We painfully thawed, patted cold water on frostbites and peeled off excess clothing. Fingers and toes burned for an hour and were red and swollen.

Boots was delightedly making herself to home. Narciss loves animals, and they all adore him and follow him around. It is comical to see him with the horses, cattle, sheep, ducks, chickens and pigs that they keep at Clayton. Most of them are loose and they all follow Narciss around like the hen and her brood.

We spent an enjoyable evening. Curly and I hadn't seen anyone since the road closed and we laughed, gossiped and listened to the radio, comfortably sleepy and lazy after the long hike and a lunch. Mrs. Druin spoke a little English, and Narciss none at all. The conversation was in French, and once in a while Curly caught the drift of it and started talking in English. He and Narciss soon found themselves in a complicated discussion, each gesturing and thinking the other must surely understand— Curly talking about the road, and Narciss about his horses, both in perfect agreement.

Mrs. Druin and I laughed until our sides ached, and when we had translated their remarks, they looked at each other, grinned, and started again, this time reversing subjects.

A curious thing I have noticed is that a funny story in English never sounds funny when it is told in French. The same is true of a French story told in English.

The next morning we ate a hearty breakfast, collected letters to be mailed and started down the road again. The weather was mild and clear, and we soon took off our parkas and snowshoed in shirtsleeves, willing to wager anything that a plane would come today.

Weather changes rapidly in the St. John Valley because it is partly influenced by the St. Lawrence River. We always used to listen to the weather reports on the radio, and if they said clear and ceiling unlimited, it would be blowing a living gale where we were. This day was mild, and I'll bet they were catching a devilish cold spell on the Penobscot.

The snow was sticky and damp when the sun had warmed it, and our snowshoes were wet and heavy. We frequently stopped to rest, dug the snowballs from Boots's paws, munched on the cheese Mrs. Druin had put in my pocket, and smoked a cigarette. It was fourteen miles to the St. John River and Nine Mile where we planned to spend the night, and after every mile I was sure it was dinnertime. I tried to convince Curly that it was, but he never relented until we were at the old lumber camp about two miles from Nine Mile.

We built a fire in the rickety box stove in the office, boiled snow water for tea, and lounged on the rough board bunk that was covered with dry fir boughs. Mrs. Druin had given us a lunch, and after eating I was sleepy and comfortable, and could have stayed there.

"Come on," Curly urged. "It's only two miles to Nine Mile."

"This is a good place to stay. It's nice and warm." I poured another cup of tea into the battered tin cup we had found.

"It may not be so warm tonight."

"All right, Simon Legree." I stood up and groaned, and felt a thousand years old.

"Listen!"

"It's a plane! They did come!"

We went outside and saw it overhead.

"Too late now." I strapped on my snowshoes and harnessed Boots again.

By midafternoon we passed the lumber camp at the St. John River and stopped to talk a while with the trappers, to give them our news for theirs before going on across the bridge to the game warden's camp at Nine Mile. The camp was set in a hollow near the bridge, and snowdrifts had piled so high around the porch that we had to dig a tunnel to get through to the door. It was deadly cold inside and I crawled into a sleeping bag on the couch while Curly built fires in both stoves and opened all the doors.

We raided the larder; had hot biscuits and canned salmon for supper, and made biscuit and salmon sandwiches for our lunch the next day.

The next morning I felt grand. All the soreness was gone from my muscles; I felt that I could walk for miles and miles. The day was crisper, and a biting wind was blowing. Snowshoes swished on the light crust. Snow slid from spruce boughs with a rustling whisper, and a high wind raced the light clouds across the sky, faintly moaning through the treetops.

I like to snowshoe. It is like waltzing, swinging from the hips in long strides, and not just picking them up and laying them down as I have heard it described. It is faster than a walk, with the body slightly bent forward, as though the weight of it carried you along. Arms are loose and breathing is even.

We left the protective green wood and were almost through the eight-mile stretch of hideous burnt land—a destructive waste and a constant reminder of the dangers of forest fires. For mile upon mile there was nothing but grim, barren, blackened trees, some upright and others lying crisscross as they had fallen.

I had things other than forest fires to think about: the hot bath and good food awaiting us. I hadn't called a halt since we'd started, and my stomach was so empty I had to hold my pants up to keep them on.

"When do we eat?" I howled.

Curly never stopped. I was sure he wasn't that deaf. "WHEN DO WE EAT?" That stopped him.

"You don't want to eat here."

"I'll eat anywhere as long as it's soon."

"Can't you wait until we get to Lac Frontiere and have a good feed?"

"What! And starve to death in the meantime? I want to eat now!" I sat down, determined not to be moved with dynamite.

We built a fire under a blowdown, propped up a stick to hold the tea pail of snow, and there we were—home again. The biscuit and salmon sandwiches were frozen, and we toasted them over the flames. The outside was hot and soft, but the inside was still hard. The tea was scalding and strong enough to float a spike, but I'd have eaten the fur off my parka had it been served on a piece of birch bark.

After a rest and a cigarette, we started over the last five miles of ridges. In the green wood again we were sheltered from the nippy wind, and I was refreshed and tireless when we topped the last hill and looked down over Canada. This was a different scene. Here were small villages, a few wood lots, and a gleaming spired church in the distance. The church reflected the direct rays of the sun, and I used to wonder what it could be made of, to shine so. One day we drove through the village and I was disappointed to find the church covered with an ugly metal sheeting.

The Bridges were staying at the hotel in Lac Frontiere, and they met us at the American customhouse. We started talking, and we talked until we were through the Canadian customs and were walking over town. Cook Poulin, proprietor of the hotel in Lac Frontiere, greeted us at the door. He was grinning from ear to ear, and his round waistline jiggled with suppressed laughter.

"Saturday night, Curlee. Bean for supper!"

Curly roared. "By the holy sailor! Cook, if you show me any beans, I'll jump down your throat and gallop your guts out!"

Cook really had a magnificent feast ready for us. We had roast chicken with giblet gravy, buttered carrots and string beans, mashed potatoes, lettuce, ripe tomatoes, fresh milk and ice cream—prepared as only incomparable Cook can do it. Curly and I quietly plucked the plump fowl clean.

It was pleasant to be staying at the hotel. I learned to knit stockings, bought yarn for a sweater, stopped at every little store to see what they had, and called on friends. There were no dishes to wash, and only our room to look after. We had three meals a day and we didn't have to get up in the morning to build a fire. We could take a bath when we felt like it—that is, we could if there was any hot water left.

Everyone in Lac Frontiere was having *la grippe* that winter, and two died. There was no doctor there that year and no government nurse as there usually is. The nearest doctor was in St. Camille, twenty miles away, with the road closed. There was a veterinary in St. Pamphile, thirty miles away, and that road was also closed. Curly and Mrs. Bridges both had *la grippe*, and I fed them castor oil and put them to bed. For days they raced back and forth along the corridor to get to the bathroom, but it wasn't long before they could join Bridgie and me in the dining room.

Chapter 17

Lac Frontiere

We spent three weeks at the hotel, and we wanted to go home. With Bridgie off scaling long lumber in St. Adelbert on the boundary, there was no one Curly could talk to. He sat in the hotel lobby and listened to the "lounge lizards."

"Listen to them," he growled. "You can't tell me they understand what they're saying."

He puzzled over the comic page in a Quebec newspaper, then brought it to me to be translated. It was the first time I knew that Tarzan was a Frenchman, and it didn't seem natural for Mutt and Jeff to be saying, "Bonjour, Mutt," and "Bonjour, Jeff."

The Lac Frontiere priest appeared at the hotel one day, soliciting for a poor family in his parish. He was an Irishman, but his native language was French, and he often joked about it. Though the man was genial, I don't think that he was happy. The poverty and need of the people in his church were reflected in his thin, lined face and nervous energy. That day he was in search of a cradle for a newborn youngster on the range roads. At the time, the baby was occupying a huge kettle, hung close to the rafters of the cabin, where the air was warmer.

When you are in Rome, they say, do as the Romans do. We tried to do that in Lac Frontiere. Dancing was frowned upon by the church, so when we had a dance at Lac Frontiere, it was not a dance for the people of the village. Cook, the proprietor of the hotel, was only too glad to let the American people take possession, but the natives of the town did not mingle with us at such affairs. And yet we were not ostracized. The people were friendly, and most of them were only too glad to see us coming.

Though these dances at Lac Frontiere were small, private affairs, we had wonderful times. On one occasion we hired musicians from St. Marcel, two violins and a banjo. Cook cleared the tables out of the dining room and sometimes we danced in the huge kitchen. There usually weren't more than twenty or thirty of us, but it was a get-together when the road was open, and recreation.

With only six of us at the hotel that winter, ourselves, the Bridges and the Nine Mile game warden and his wife, we played poker to pass away the long evenings.

A plane came to Churchill and we telephoned for it to come after us. We loaded the baggage compartment with a two months' supply of groceries, put Boots in and waved good-bye, glad to have been out, and glad to go home again.

It was snowing lightly and the pilot flew low over the tree-tops, following the road. The trees were so close I thought I could reach through the broken windowpane and grab a branch. Boots gave us a fright when she decided she didn't like to ride in an airplane and scrambled over us trying to get out through the broken window. Curly had to hang onto the door handle to keep the door closed, and we had quite a struggle before I could get the dog muzzled and quieted. In half an hour we taxied up Umsaskis Lake—and I remembered that it had taken us two and a half days to walk out.

We thought the road would be open by the fifteenth of April, but from the first to the twelfth it snowed every day, adding two more feet of snow to what we already had, and burying the stick I had set out to see how fast it melted.

We really didn't mind. We had enough food and I had bought egg powders at Lac Frontiere that were quite all right to cook with. After the twelfth of April, the days were warm and sunny. Snow melted all day and the porch was dry enough to sit on. We basked in the warm sun and listened to the water drip from the roof.

Every late afternoon we walked down to the main road to where the car was kept in a garage. As the snow melted away in the sunshiny spot in front of the garage, we backed the car out into the road and drove ten feet. It was quite grand, and quite exciting to actually ride. Every day we drove a few feet further, and although we knew we couldn't possibly get through the snowdrifts with the small coupé, we could still do a lot of wishful thinking.

To me, April always seems to be the longest month in the year. I like the summertime, but I'm glad when fall comes. I like to see winter come too, especially the first snowstorm. I even like to be snowbound, and I think I actually feel relieved when January rolls around and the road is closed. February is a cold month and March is pleasant, but April is betwixt and between. Winter doesn't go fast enough and spring doesn't come soon enough. It is the sensation of waiting that I dislike.

Bridgie started from Lac Frontiere with his light truck, and on May fourth he came as far as Clayton Lake. Narciss opened the road to Churchill. The telephone rang insistently, and when they went by Umsaskis we were at the main road, ready to go. Some of the drifts that had been shoveled through were still four feet deep, but once the sun shone on the tracks, the snow melted.

Almost everyone in the country met at Clayton Lake for his mail. After the long winter's isolation there was an enormous collection of letters, packages, newspapers and new catalogues to be sorted over and read. Practically the first words anyone was greeted with were, "My, but you are thin!"

I think everyone lost weight that winter, especially myself, Anna Deblois and Madelain Druin. It was our initiation. Most woods people are skinny anyway. When I first went to Churchill I weighed a hundred and forty pounds, and after two months of Mrs. Deblois's cooking, I weighed a hundred and sixty! That winter at Umsaskis I weighed a hundred and eight, and that summer, a hundred and twenty, a weight that has never varied since then. Curly claims that he was swindled. He bargained for a size thirty-eight, and now he has a beanpole.

Chapter 18

Spring Fever

Spring came at last. Nature pushed back her blanket and revealed little blades of green in last year's brown, soggy soil. The wind was soft and moisture laden, stealing away the last remnants of white snow. The sun was hot and close, warming through woolen clothes and tanning cheeks and foreheads. Barren trees were lightly nobbed and tinged with sticky, yellowish-green buds that burst forth with the joy of living into tiny leaves as big as a mouse's ear, a spreading, growing and rippling garment, flashing, dancing and preening in the sun. The dowdy evergreens were not to be outdone, and they too showed their light shoots—a green moiré delicately tipping every branch and twig. The blue depths of the sky were infinite. We were lethargic and sleepy, lounging on the porch steps and indulging in spring fever, intoxicated with the heady air and unwilling to eat or work, only wishing to sleep and sleep.

In the old days when a lad drowsed in the spring sun with half-closed eyelids, he was treated with sulphur and molasses for a blood cleansing. But what could be more refreshing than that short, somnolent, castle-building period that is filled with suppressed excitement and impatience for the swimming hole to warm up. We were waiting for the ice to go out so we could go fishing.

The bread crumbs and cornmeal that we spread around the camp had brought us many wild creatures, and more different kinds of birds than I knew existed. I presumed a game warden knew all about the birds, beasts, and wild flowers of the forests, and I asked Curly what each new bird was.

"It's a cedar waxwing," he declared.

"What is that one with the yellow markings?"

"That's a cedar waxwing."

I smelled a rat. "What is that?" I pointed to a blue jay.

"Cedar waxwing," he stated firmly.

They were all "cedar waxwings"!

The most interesting thing to me were the flocks of young partridges along the road. We didn't see them often because they were so tiny, but we drove slowly and carefully along the road, watching for a mother hen. If we stopped the car quickly and jumped out, we sometimes saw a flurry of fuzzy, yellow chicks about the size of a half dollar, scattering to hide under a leaf, behind a blade of grass or under the mother partridge's wing.

Once they were in the leaves they were as quiet as snowflakes, but the hen partridge was angry and outraged. She clucked loudly, rushed up and down the road, first toward us and then away, dragging a wing along the ground and limping to induce us to follow her and draw danger away from her chicks.

One day we drove up to a partridge that was sitting in the middle of the road. Curly stopped the car about ten feet away from her and tooted the horn. She sputtered and arched her head, spread her wings and angrily flew at the car, struck the windshield and fell on the hood. It was then I noticed the dozen chicks that ran in all directions like little clouds of dust whirling away.

Mother hen jumped off the hood of the car and scuttled for the side of the road, running back and forth, edging further away from the chicks and finally disappearing when they had vanished in the tall grass.

Strangers that came into the country were careless about the young flocks and ran into them before they saw them. We found one dead hen with seven little ones pitifully fluttering around it and trying to get under the wing. Curly stepped out of the car, sent the chicks running into the grass, and took the dead bird away.

"The chicks will die!" I protested.

"I think another flock will adopt them," he said. "But I'd like a word with the screwball that ran into this one."

Two days later, in the same place in the road, we saw a hen and sixteen chicks, her own and the adopted ones.

The only chick I ever inspected closely was a little one we had found in the road. A car had struck it and both tiny legs were broken. Curly killed it instantly, as it is practically impossible to raise them in captivity. It was so tiny I could close my hand over the little thing. Whenever we met any of the fishermen coming in for the spring fishing I warned them about the young flocks. They had never noticed them and had probably passed twenty or thirty different flocks.

As the chicks grow older they lose that fuzzy, yellow color, and dark feathers show the outlines of wings and ruff. They are bolder and not so quick to heed the mother's warning cluck. They can't all squeeze under the wing, and tails and heads stick out, wriggling and beady eyed. By the time they are as big as the domesticated barnyard chick that is still yellow, the baby partridge is a small replica of the parent birds.

One summer a flock of partridges lived in our dooryard. When they were tiny we didn't see them often, but as they grew older we saw them wandering around the edges of the porch, walking on the railing, or perched on the canoe rack. Mother hen was in the midst of them, watching everywhere, picking up small pieces of gravel on the lawn, the chicks imitating her.

They seemed to be quite tame, even when we went outside for a better look at them, and we could get within a few feet of them before they moved away. On rainy mornings they would be there, huddled under the car, in the garage, and strangely enough, eating the remains of Boots's dog mash left in the dish.

The most arresting sight I ever saw on the road was a doe and two wobbly, spotted fawns, one on either side of her. They walked along leisurely with heads bent and their short, bushy tails swinging back and forth, never looking to right or left, and daintily stepping over the rutted road. We came upon them suddenly, and for some time they didn't notice the car. We followed slowly, trying to keep as far behind as possible, but the doe lifted her head and turned to look. She whirled and leaped into the bushes with the baby fawns right behind her. We saw many fawns in the cedar swamps along the road, but nothing as unconsciously charming as those twins.

While driving twenty miles one night, we counted as many as a hundred rabbits. "Look at 'em go!" Curly shouted. "Looks like popcorn!"

We saw little porcupines with their fine quills, and we once saw a young bobcat that was no bigger than a kitten. Small foxes were funny and awkward. They watched us until we were close to them, then they ran ahead of the car. We didn't like them because young as they were, they were hunting for partridge chicks. No woodsman likes Reynard the Fox, but I think most of that is due to his wise, smirking expression.

I did like to see the old she-bear in the burnt land with her cubs. She must have weighed four hundred pounds but she bounced across the road like an overgrown rubber ball. The cubs followed behind as we counted—one, two, three. They were like chubby teddy bears. We saw them in the burnt land for a year, and then the old she-bear was alone again. They are pesty creatures in the springtime when they are hungry, and everyone in the country has "bear trouble."

A bear climbed into Mrs. Paquet's pigpen at Churchill and raked his claws over the pig's back before they could drive him away. The next evening he broke through a boardinghouse window. Mrs. Deblois and Anna were sitting in the living room, and when they heard the window crash, Mrs. Deblois went to see what it was. She turned on the light and there was Bruin with both front paws in the sink. She ran outside to call Joe Deblois, but the bear escaped before they could shoot him.

The hermit at Knowles Brook on the St. John River shot a bear breaking into his camp, and Conrad Poulin at Seven Islands shot a bear in his barn. Cyril was in his camp at Umsaskis when a bear stepped onto the porch and pushed the door open. He shot at him and missed. Mrs. Bridges shot a bear near their camp.

The funniest bear incident occurred at Clayton Lake. Narciss Druin had seven men working for him at Clayton, and they slept in one of the small camps on the edge of the woods. During the night the door opened, and one of the men awoke. He arose and closed the door with a slam, and had no sooner turned his back when the door banged open again, this time with vehemence. The fellow turned around and faced a huge black bear standing in the doorway.

That was too much. He dashed down the lane between the sleepers, and dove headfirst through the back window. The bear was right behind him and they raced across a clearing, he in his long underwear and the bear pounding at his heels. Luckily the door at Druins' house was unlocked, and the man bounced inside, awoke the startled couple and jabbered out his story. Narciss went back with a gun but the bear had gone.

When the rest of the men awakened and learned that a bear had been through the camp without their knowing it, they were ready to go home.

A bear broke into the mailman's camp at Clayton. He tore down the door, smashed all the furniture, tipped over the stove, broke open all the canned goods and ate the contents. He drank the molasses from the jug—and this is true. He did leave the windowpanes intact—and a ten-inch paw print on one of them.

Curly didn't get away scot-free. He lost three canoes, one on Priestly and two on Chemquassabamticook Lake. Whenever we went fishing we were careful not to let the fish touch the canoe, but someone had used the canoes and hadn't been as careful. When the bears located the fish smell, they tore the canoes to shreds and scattered the pieces for half a mile around.

Bear stories are good because they are so human. Did you ever hear the one about the party of hunters who surrounded a bear? The only man in the crowd who didn't have a gun was the old guide, and Bruin broke through the circle by toppling over him. It was a good joke on the guide, and the sportsmen ragged him plenty. "Pete, what did that bear say to you when he was whispering in your ear?"

Pete scratched his head. "Wall, I'll tell ye. He says, 'Son, don't send no boys out to do a man's job.' "

I don't like bear meat, first because it smells and second because I can't forget the first bear I ever helped skin. It looked like a man hanging up. When people tell me that bear meat is good, I ask them if they ever fed it to a dog. Dogs won't eat bear meat—not because the meat isn't good, but because they dislike the smell of bears.

I very seldom saw bears while I was walking in the woods, probably because I am a noisy hunter. The bear always saw me first, and all I ever saw were his tracks.

The first and only time I ever saw a moose, and had a good look at him, I was driving to Lac Frontiere alone in the car. I almost ran into him as I came around a sharp curve. I slammed on the brakes and stopped within five feet of him.

He was the most formidable thing I cared to see, and had it been September, I'm sure he would have charged the car as moose have been known to do. For a minute I thought he was going to. My hands gripped the steering wheel, and I held my breath and leaned forward to get a full-length view of him. He towered over the car, long legged, knobby kneed, ungainly and dark. His head was lowered and he stared at me. He wasn't pretty but his eyes were brown and soft looking. He had no antlers yet, but the huge bell, a saclike appendage of loose hide beneath his chin, identified him as a bull moose.

It seemed as though he stood in the road for half an hour without moving, but in reality it was only a few minutes. I gathered enough courage to toot the horn, and he merely swung around and trotted up the road. I followed with the car for half a mile before he turned off into the tangle of burnt land.

I would like to see one some time with his fall spread of antlers. Moose are awe inspiring enough without them, and with their enormous antlers they must be quite majestic. I have heard their call in September, but I wouldn't describe it as a "call." It is halfway between a cough and a grunt.

Chapter 19

Trout and Togue

Finally the ice went out of Umsaskis Lake and Churchill Lake, and Curly thought it wouldn't be long before it went out of Eagle Lake too. We packed the outboard motor, gasoline can, grub box, sleeping bags and fishing tackle into the back of the car and drove to Churchill.

It was a perfect day for the ice to "run." The weather was raw, cold and windy, and every wave that broke against the bow of the canoe sent a shower of spray back on to us.

We went ten miles through Churchill Lake and into the thoroughfare and Eagle Lake. The ice had shifted out of the cove and the rest of the lake was still full, but from the way the wind was blowing, we knew the ice would be out before night. A game warden's camp was across the cove, and we went over to start a fire, dry out a bit, and inspect the camp to see how it had withstood the winter.

We trolled a while off the ledge near the narrows, running the motor slowly and letting out hand lines with a daredevil lure—a red-and-white-striped spoon with three hooks, sometimes called a barber pole. The spoon wobbles and looks like a minnow flashing as it is pulled through the water about thirty feet behind the canoe. We were fishing for togue, or lake trout—the largest of trout—also called laker, namaycush or gray trout. I had never heard them called anything but togue until a party of fishermen proudly showed us their catch of "gray trout."

"But those are togue," I said, putting my foot in it that time.

"Oh, no, these are gray trout!" they replied, outraged.

To me, trout meant the colorful, flashy brook trout, or squaretail. Curly assured me that the fishermen were right. Togue are trout, even though they are grayish and silvery and not as colorful and "fighting" a fish as the squaretail.

I had the first strike and landed a four-and-a-half-pound togue. Strikes came fast and furiously after that, and no sooner had Curly unhooked one and thrown it back, when I was busy pulling in another. We kept the first one I'd caught and one of the smallest of the others to have in a chowder for dinner.

It was bitterly cold on the lake, and we went back to camp. My woolen mittens were soaking wet, and the spray had run off the brim of my fishing hat and down the back of my neck. I didn't notice it. I was too excited. I had never been togue fishing before, and it seemed almost impossible that there could be so many of them. I groaned every time Curly let one go. He chuckled and said, "Well, that one ought to weigh six or seven pounds anyway."

Togue make excellent chowder when skinned and boiled in a kettle of water, then boned and the meat separated into large flakes. Onions and potatoes are cooked in the fish water, and little squares of salt pork are fried and added to it with the flaked fish and milk. I don't as a rule like my chowder too thick, but the best fish chowder I ever ate was cooked in layers—a layer of potatoes, a layer of onions, a layer of fish, potatoes and so on, with just enough fish water and milk to cook them.

After dinner we went out again and watched the ice pounding to pieces on the shores. We rode through the narrows and into Russell Cove when it moved out of there, and we trolled along the ledge shore, getting strikes all along. Curly cut two hooks from the daredevil lure and filed the barb from the third, and during the day's fishing we caught and liberated twenty-eight togue, the largest probably weighing eleven pounds. I thought it was a deadhead, a water-soaked log, when I pulled it up to the canoe gunwale. "Don't you touch it!" I howled.

"You don't want *that*!" Curly said. "Look at it, it's bigger than the canoe."

"Don't want it! Well I guess I do. I'll never catch another one that big!"

"You have two fish and you don't want this one." Curly was adamant. "It would be just a waste of fish. We'd never be able to eat it before it spoiled."

The biggest togue I've seen caught in Eagle Lake weighed eighteen pounds. Curly caught one that was twisted like a corkscrew. A fish hawk or an eagle had picked it up when it was young and had broken its back in several places. It still had deep scars from the wounds the claws had made.

There is an eagle's nest in a high tree at the mouth of Russell Brook, and the eagles were out fishing too, swooping low over the water and flying back to their nests with a fish. Joe Giguare had some mink sets on Eagle Lake and accidentally caught an eagle in one of them. When the eagle swooped down to get the fish that was used as bait, he sprang the trap and was caught. It was still alive when Joe found it, and it struggled so hard he had to kill it with a twenty-two rifle to get it out of the trap. It stretched seven feet from wing tip to wing tip, and its legs were as big around as a man's wrist.

Other lures are as good as the daredevil. The Davis spoon, large and golden with little red beads, is popular. There is a mother-of-pearl spoon with a little red dot on the inside. When the spoon spins, the dot changes to a line. In the spring the best bait for togue is "sewn" bait—live bait that is four or five inches long and sewn on a gut hook, looped first through the head, the hook caught in the side, and twisted a bit so the bait will wobble and seem alive.

We rode home by starlight. The lake was calm, but the air was raw and chilly. I crawled into the sleeping bag in the bottom of the canoe, and the purr of the motor soon put me to sleep. We had three togue with us and left many more that wouldn't touch a daredevil lure, but would just grow fat and lazy and stay in deep water.

During the hot summer months togue fishing isn't good. Trout and togue are deep where it is cool. They can be caught by plug fishing off the ledges with pieces of salt pork or ten-inch chub. The largest togue are caught that way, and they are so big the description of them sounds like a fish story.

There are no salmon in Eagle, Chamberlain, Churchill, Umsaskis, Long, Clayton or Chemquassabamticook lakes. A few were stocked in Priestly Lake, and sometimes one is caught. Allagash is trout country, with muddy shoals and cold brooks, and there are plenty of squaretails and lakers. Eagle Lake is best for togue fishing, but other lakes will yield a daily limit. A few hours on Eagle Lake are all that are needed to get a ten-pound limit.

There are several good trout brooks that enter Eagle Lake. From the fifteenth to the last day of May—before black-fly time—the only trout fishing in the country at that time is on Soper Brook. I was wild with excitement the first time I fished there. We paddled up the brook to the old log dam, beached the canoe below the rips and walked up to the dam with our rods and bait. There is only one bait the trout will rise to and that is a small minnow, not more than two inches long and sewn with a tiny gut hook. Curly had been there before and he tried the first cast to show me how it was done. He walked out on the slime-covered boom log, dropped the bait just below the dam where the rapids begin, and let out twenty feet of line.

The first strike was sharp and lost the bait. He sewed another on and hooked the next fish with a sharp jerk. I bounced up and down on the bank. "You're going to lose it! Hurry up, I want to try it! Look out! You're going to fall in! Don't lose it! Ah-h-h!" I breathed a sigh of relief when it was lying in the moss, a beautiful squaretail that weighed two pounds.

I lost three fish before I could land one—another two-pound trout—and we caught three more before I fell into the pool. That was the end of fishing, and we would have to wait until next year at the same time to catch any more of those spotted beauties from that pool.

When the leaves are budding and the black flies are as thick as raindrops, the fishing is good everywhere. There are monster-sized trout below Churchill dam if the sluice gates are closed, but it is a ticklish job to catch them. They take flies or worms and will lead an Izaak Walton on a merry chase between the boulders and in the swift water.

Long Lake dam is another fisherman's paradise. Black flies never bother Curly, and the first time he took me there, he forgot the fly dope. I was stationed just to the side of the sluice way where I could throw my lowly worm into the rips, and about that time the pesky mosquitoes, black flies and nosee-ums found me and I was busy. The trout were biting and so were the flies. My worm supply was diminishing, and I had to use pieces of worms, and finally the red-bottomed fin from one of the trout I'd caught. I wished that old witch *Pook-jin-skwess*—who changed herself into a mosquito to pester mankind—was in Hades.

I never caught trout like that, one right after the other. Curly grinned from ear to ear when I had a bite on both ends.

"What's the matter, Pooie, got ants in your pants?"

"You wait!" I threatened. "When I get home and get my hands on that fly dope, I'll make you drink it!"

Within an hour I had my limit—twenty-five trout from seven to ten inches long—and I ran back to the caretaker's camp, shaking out the midges that were buzzing in my hair. My face and hands swelled until I looked like a bloated scarecrow. Salt and water took out most of the sting, but I must have had a good inoculation because they didn't bother me as much after that.

There is only one thing to be wished for in the woods—that there be no black flies. Curly made a fly dope of tar, turpentine, citronella—and dissolved horseshoes, I guess. It kept the flies away for a while, but it also peeled the hide off. I preferred a net over my head and shoulders, with my sleeves buttoned tightly and my pants legs tucked into wading shoes. Even then the nosee-ums crawled through the buttonholes and set my skin on fire.

After the first meal of trout in the spring, I've had my fill. Curly could eat them three times a day. He chews on them as he does corn on the cob, gnawing off skin, fins and flesh, and leaving the bones. I get so tired of trout, a juicy hamburger would be wonderful.

We never spoiled trout by rolling them in cornmeal, but wiped them dry and fried them in hot salt-pork fat, turning frequently to keep them from curling. The scramble came when the "gri-ads"—the golden squares of salt pork—were done. Curly snitched them every time, and I finally divided them, putting half on the table with the fish and half in a little bowl to be eaten when he was looking for more.

Big trout aren't as tasty as the little ones that are about seven or eight inches long. A four- or five-pounder takes too long to cook and isn't as sweet tasting. I baked them with a stuffing of bread crumbs, melted butter and Worcestershire sauce.

One time Curly took my brother fishing on Umsaskis Lake. They caught a lot of trout but kept throwing them back because they were too big. Carl was dismayed. He had never caught three- or four-pounders and he wanted some evidence to back up the fish story. Curly let him keep three of them, and on the way back to camp they met a fishing party with no fish. Curly gave them the two biggest ones and Carl had one three-pounder left to bring home.

There were a lot of times when we especially wanted a few trout, and then it was impossible to catch them anywhere, usually when we had company that we'd been bragging to about the fishing. We did have good luck one time. Four friends were staying with us one weekend, and the usual argument was brought up: Who could catch the most trout, the women or the men? Curly went to Sebemsicook Stream on Long Lake with his two cronies, and one of the other women and I went to Drake Brook. We caught thirty trout to the men's twenty.

Curly was going to take the men down the St. John River the next day, so we arose early, drove to the St. John River, took the canoe from the forks on Nine Mile Brook, and fished down the St. John River. By the time they caught up with us, we had stopped at every spring hole, and were down to Four Mile Brook, ready to go home with our limit. We saw them coming.

"Hide the fish, Eve. Here they come. Hi!" I yelled to them. "Any luck?"

"Just four." Curly held up their catch. "How did you get down here?" They didn't seem very pleased to see us.

"Setting pole," I said, condescendingly.

"If you cut that canoe you'll have to patch it." They were suspicious now. We looked much too self-satisfied.

"Give us a tow home?" I asked.

"Thought we'd fish a while, but I guess the water's too low." Curly snubbed their canoe nearer us. "Guess we'll go to Eagle. I don't suppose you caught any?" They watched us closely.

"A few. Show 'em, Eve. Guess that will hold you."

In the early spring we used worms to catch trout, but most of the time we used wet flies—the Parmachenee Belle, the Brown Hackle, the Gray Hackle, the Silver Doctor, and the Mickey Finn. Curly prefers streamer flies and has good luck with them. Curiously enough, a lot of people think that the flies used for fishing are supposed to represent flies. Actually, the streamer flies represent little fish—the Gray Ghost, for instance, looks like a little smelt. Other flies are lures. The Parmachenee Belle was made to look like the red-and-white-bottomed fin of a trout.

I don't know much about fly fishing, and the first time I ever used a fly rod was a great strain on Curly's good nature. We went to the head of Umsaskis one evening in September, and I had a new three-ounce fly rod that was whippy and much too light for me. I accidentally let my Parmachenee Belle drop on the water and a trout grabbed it. I threw the rod in the water and started pulling in the line, hand over hand, growing wilder every second. Curly made a few casts and caught two. I lashed forth in real movie style, whipping the water to a froth.

His advice was, "Sufferin' lucivees! Keep your elbow down! That isn't a setting pole! Oh, my sainted aunt! It's in my ears!"

"If your ears didn't stick out so far they wouldn't be caught!"

"SIT DOWN! Before I hit you with a paddle! And stop your sassing! Those fish will be there when you get untangled."

Over our heads sailed a trout. I yanked so hard I nearly fell out of the canoe.

It is fun to go fishing, no worries, no bother, and half of the fun is riding in a canoe or wading up a brook. Even a cold lunch of dry biscuits and peanut butter tastes good, and if it is a sunny day, I'd rather sleep in the bottom of the canoe—that is, if the fish aren't biting.

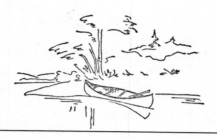

Chapter 20

Downriver

When the novelty of spring fishing wears off, we devote our time to going downriver. Going outside to civilization is going downriver to the people living on the Allagash and St. John rivers. If they go in the opposite direction, through Canada and Jackman, Maine, it is still going downriver.

I felt out of place when we made our few trips outside. We usually left at a moment's notice, and once on the road we talked and talked, writing down a list of things we wanted to buy.

"Better get some adhesive tape," Curly suggested.

"Whatever do you do with all the tape? Oh, I know, I wanted some liquid stockings."

"Some what?" Curly pricked up his ears.

"Liquid stockings. I heard about it on the radio. You paint your legs to look like stockings."

"I never heard of that. I'd look cute in liquid stockings. I suppose ten years from now I'll be wearing a straw hat and a summer union suit in forty-below weather, and think nothing of it."

"This isn't for you, this is for me. We also need some jar rubbers for those fiddlehead greens." We had just picked two bushels of fiddlehead greens—those very young ferns that are curled up like the head of a violin. They grow in the marsh and we pick them just as they sprout through the moist soil, and cook them much the same as any green vegetable—in salty water, or add a piece of salt pork. They are more tasty cold than hot, and we usually ate them with vinegar that had been exposed to garlic. We canned what we had left over.

Curly wore his best uniform that we kept wrapped in a sheet all winter for just this occasion, and I wore silk stockings that itched, a hat that bothered me, and a pair of gloves that I hated to wear. When we crossed the boundary into Maine again, we could hardly wait until we reached Jackman, stopped in front of a drugstore, cashed a check for some American money and bought two triple-deck cones of ice cream—vanilla, chocolate and strawberry. We stopped everywhere, in every town that we went through, ate at lunch counters and restaurants, and called on friends.

We once spent two days in Bangor—the Maine lumberjack's Mecca. We went to a dance, a movie, a bowling alley, the Chinese restaurants and the sporting-goods stores. We ate scallops, clams and lobsters for breakfast, dinner and supper. I was always tempted to order crepes suzettes—"drunken pancakes" as Cyril calls them—but I never got around to it, and I still don't know what they taste like. We did buy Cuban cigarettes that tasted like cigars.

I enjoyed it, but I could never shake off the feeling that the world was crowded and that people were odd. Cosmetics, especially, were glaring. Curly said I was the one who was woods queer, but I wondered about that when I read the papers and listened to the gossip. It isn't the "Moosetowner" that stares at a new style in hats. He takes things as a matter of course and deals with them in his own particular way.

The first Model-T Ford seen in Allagash was owned by Tom Gardner, a native of the village, who gingerly drove it over rutted dirt roads. One wet day when the roads were greasy with reddish mud, he set forth to crank Lizzie, and left the throttle open. Lizzie sputtered, snorted and leaped forward, ran over Tom, and rattled, crashed and rocketed up the hill. Tom got up, bewildered but unhurt. The Ford spun on the slippery hill and hurtled back, knocked Tom down again and sailed over him.

This time Tom bounced into the house and reappeared on the scene with a double-barreled shotgun. He was fighting mad and feather white.

"By the ram-cattin', bobtailed, yelpin', cater-wailin' Injun Devils! I'll fix ye this time!"

He did with both charges, and Lizzie coughed and choked to a standstill with an engineful of buckshot.

Going downriver may be one of the pleasant phases of spring fever, but spring housecleaning isn't. I put everything off until the last minute, but when the day came for the Red Sox to play the Yankees for their first game of the season, I dropped a bombshell. "Better houseclean today."

Curly opened one eye, gingerly put his feet onto the floor, and sat up. "Well, that's all right. I've got to go in and see Louie Paquet today."

"You're not going anywhere. If you do you'll miss the game. Take these mattresses and pillows outside and give them a good shaking."

He poked around in the junk I had piled in the middle of the floor. "What's this?" He picked up a "contraption."

"Oh, nothing."

"But what is it?"

"Just a machine to roll yarn with." I was busy washing logs.

"Where did you get it?" He always asks the silliest questions.

"I made it."

"Does it work?"

Damn. "No, of course it never worked, and don't stand there grinning. The windowpane is broken. Bring in the dustpan and the broom. This fish oil leaked all over the place, and I need two more pails of water."

"But the bases are loaded and Ted Williams is coming to bat!"

This was revenge. "I'll tell you about it when you get back. Oh! My lamp chimney! That beautiful lamp chimney! I'll never be able to replace it!"

Nothing gets as dusty and cluttery as a camp. The dirt that is used for insulating between the roofs sifts through constantly. Logs are greasy and black behind the kitchen stove where hot fat spatters, and they have to be scrubbed with lye and a brush. There is never enough closet room, and clothes collect on trunks, tables and in corners. I hate to throw anything away as I am sure to want it later. Curly picks up everything he can find and stores it in the garage. Old tacks are priceless. Someone else might want the old books and magazines. A broken paddle handle makes a good stick to stir boiling clothes with, and tobacco cans are just the thing to carry worms in. A piece of wire will patch anything, from broken chair legs to split paddle blades, or hold the stovepipe in place.

By midafternoon we had reached the cupboards. "Take all this stuff and dump it in the lake."

"The vermicelli too?"

"Yes, the vermicelli too."

"But it is still good!" he protested.

"It may be still good, but it smells funny. You've had it since you were at Eagle Lake. What ever did you buy so much for? You had better blacken the kitchen stove now, and I'll warm the beans on the outdoor fireplace."

"Do we have *beans* again for supper?" Curly howled.

When cleaning was done, Curly was ready to collapse. Half my fingers were bandaged, and the camp smelled clean because of the strong yellow soap we had used to scrub the logs and woodwork with. The cupboards looked empty and we could get into the bedroom without having to force the door open.

I painted, waxed, made new curtains and a couch cover, and our spring housecleaning was finished.

"Looks nice, Pooie," Curly commented. "But when are you going to wash your overalls?"

"Do I have to wash them again? I washed them once last fall."

"If you don't wash them," he threatened, "some dark night they will walk off and leave you."

I soaked them in the lake with a piece of soap in one pocket, anchored them to the bottom with a big rock and let them "wash" for a few days. I had worn them three years, and they had just reached the "most comfortable" stage. There were but three patches on the knees and one on the seat, and they were colorfully patterned with splotches of paint.

Once the spring housecleaning was finished I had nothing to do during the rest of the summer except to laze around in the sun, fight black flies and coax Curly to take me with him on his canoe trips. A northern Maine summer is really something to look forward to. We had in our front dooryard what thousands of city people would give a great deal to enjoy—a spot of woods that only a few sportsmen could have access to.

Chapter 21

Nine Mile

That summer we moved to Nine Mile on the St. John River and Curly was given both districts to patrol. It is nine miles above Seven Islands—hence its name—and Seven Islands is ninety miles from Fort Kent, by river.

The game warden's camp was built by a former warden who had been stationed there, and he built for comfort as well as convenience. The many wardens who subsequently occupied the camp added further improvements. There was a new floor, roomy cupboards and sideboards, and new framework around windows and doors. The yard had been carefully trimmed into a lawn, each new occupant extending it until it stretched three hundred feet along the riverbank and around the camp.

"But this is amazing," strangers always remarked. "Why do you have a lawn here in the woods?"

There are two good reasons for a lawn. People who live in the woods take just as much pride in their property as city folks do, and furthermore, cutting the long grass reduces the opportunity for the black flies to multiply and pester us. Though the lawn was already extensive, we added to it ourselves and were as conscientious about keeping it trimmed as though we had done the entire work ourselves.

The log camp was large and low roofed and was divided into five rooms. The kitchen was enormous, and there was a whole wall of cupboards and sideboards. The eight-plate cookstove had a water tank on the side that heated fifteen gallons of water, and the oven was as roomy as a boxcar. The kitchen table stood in the middle of the floor, and a trapdoor and stairs descended into a large dirt cellar under the camp.

The living room was as big as the kitchen. A couch stood under a wide window, and handmade shelves and a desk were built along the front wall. Though the chairs were rickety and the bulldog stove was squat, the beautiful golden orange of shellacked woodwork blended with the mellowed logs and made the room cheery. We had enough bedrooms and beds so that we wouldn't have to use the air mattress on the kitchen floor when company came.

I liked Nine Mile camp. A porch extended across the front of the camp overlooking the lawn, the river, and the tall, slender birch trees. Pine trees shaded it. After living in two small rooms at Umsaskis, this camp seemed like a palace. Besides the main house, there was a small guest cabin, a combination garage and woodshed, and at some distance away, a deserted log cabin—a schoolhouse that had been used when large families were living there. It was a storehouse now. There is no place quite like Nine Mile. Everyone who has lived there knows the fascination of the place, its beauty and seclusion.

Curly had ample room for all his precious junk. He built a birch-bark rack on the edge of the lawn for his canoe, and he spent his time puttering in the shed and garage. It seemed wonderful to be able to lie on the lawn and bask in the sun, with no black flies around.

We were living thirty miles nearer the boundary, and we were that much closer to civilization. Now and then we could see a car drive by and occasional fishing parties going down the river. Whenever people from Churchill, Umsaskis or Clayton went out to Lac Frontiere, they stopped to call, and we saw our "neighbors" more frequently.

Since we were but fifteen miles from Lac Frontiere, we could also call the French Canadians "next-door neighbors." At first they seemed quite alien to us, more so to Curly than myself because my familiarity with their language made it easier for me to become acquainted with them.

The French Canadian is always hospitable and usually poor. No matter how lowly his hovel or how extravagantly cluttered his parlor, he is the perfect host. One must have something to eat before leaving, and enjoy a glass of homemade wine.

They make wine of almost anything—beets, dandelion flowers or potatoes. Beet wines are a deep red in color, and they are sweet and mild. The dandelion-flower wines are golden and dry, and potato wine is clear and exceedingly potent.

We once brought a friend who was quite abstemious to call on a French Canadian family, warning him that it was a social faux pas to refuse this offering of drink. The wine was not strong, but it had its effect, and he was soon in a bewildering conversation with the head of the house on the merits of a grocery store!

Lac Frontiere is a strange place. It is really a settlement that originated because of the lumbering activities on the Maine side of the boundary. There are a few houses, general stores, two hotels and a church. The railroad ends at Lac Frontiere, and there is nothing else. There is no industry, and the people live a hand-to-mouth existence. We knew Lac Frontiere quite well before we left the country and were well acquainted with most of the people.

I think my reputation in Lac Frontiere was not of the best. I wore shorts during the summer. I drove a car, smoked cigarettes and did not attend church. But worse than that, I was on speaking terms with a "fancy" lady who lived there. She had six gold teeth. Whenever I drove to Lac Frontiere for a week's supply of groceries, she would send a boy to the store with a message for me to come see her at the hotel. I would find her sitting in the "Death Chamber"—a cubbyhole of a room where liquor and ale were served—and she would be sipping straight alcohol.

"Oh, Madame Curlee, sit down. You will have something to drink? Some whisky blanc?"

"No, just a glass of ale, please."

She talked and I watched, fascinated to see anyone sip straight alcohol without wincing. After a water glass of what she called whisky blanc, the tears came and she rehearsed the latest episode in the sad story of her life.

She and the mayor planned to be married. She went to "Key-bec" to buy her trousseau, and he was to meet her within two days. She visited some friends, had a lovely time, spent all her money and was *bien soul*—well plastered for three days. The mayor was forgotten.

On the train going home, whom should she meet but the mayor who was also *bien soul*, and quite bankrupt because of his celebration. He also had met friends, and now they had to wait until they could save more money for another trip to "Key-bec."

Curly hired two Canadian boys from Lac Frontiere who agreed to cut forty face cords of wood for us. They would split it, yard it, and board themselves in the old Blanchette camp, all for the usual price—a dollar and a half a face cord. Pete and Joe

The cabin at Nine Mile Bridge where Helen and Curly spent two winters. This photo was reproduced from an unknown newspaper.

were good workers. They cut a full cord of wood a day, average $4.50 a day to split between them and feed themselves. It was an unbelievably low wage for the amount of work.

Curly was busy inspecting muskrat traps, and I hired Henri to spade the garden for us. Henri was also a Lac Frontiere boy. He was short, stocky, and swarthy and a demon for work. He arose at four in the morning, worked in the garden plot before breakfast, worked after breakfast until dinnertime, rested during the hot afternoon, and worked until dark.

He slept in the guest cabin, always being careful to make a wide detour when passing Loupe's kennel.

"Loupe is a good dog," Curly teased him. "You can have him to sleep with you, and then the bears won't get you."

"Ho no!" Henri protested. "Hi radder me she's bear den dat *chien!*"

Like all French Canadians, Henri was particular about what he ate. We had fiddlehead greens with garlic and vinegar for dinner, and he looked at them suspiciously. "You pick dat hin de swamp?" he asked.

"Sure, have some. They're good."

"I don't want some. You pipples heat funny tings."

After a day and a half of spading, a friend of his called on the telephone to inform Henri that he wished to buy a tombstone for his grandmother who had just died. Henri was the tombstone agent for Lac Frontiere, and business hadn't been so rushing for a long time. Henri departed and I finished the garden.

I planted a beautiful garden—it grew to weeds; worms ruined the string beans, and a heavy frost on the night of the Fourth of July killed the cucumbers and squash. A groundhog dug up the rest.

That summer, the St. John River bridge was having its face lifted. Narciss and a crew of men were hauling rocks from the river bed and packing them into the middle pier. When the cement mixer came to finish the job, I agreed to board the cement-mixing boss and his "aide de camp." I had my hands full. At the first meal they ate with us, I noticed that no one ate the buttered carrots or creamed peas. I passed the dish to them. "Have some vegetables?"

They looked at each other, and both spoke at once. "We do not eat vegetables."

"Don't you like them?" I asked.

One shook his head and the other patted his stomach. "I have ulcers," he explained. "There are many things I do not eat."

He drank black tea and ate two loaves of fresh bread with his meat and potatoes.

It was quite a problem to find something they did eat besides plain meat and potatoes or baked beans. I once served an extra large platter of corn bread that neither of them touched until I mentioned that it was good for stomach ulcers. (May I be forgiven!) The ulcerated one ate a piece and liked it. His companion eyed him suspiciously, then he also ate a piece and liked it. I couldn't make enough corn bread after that.

Whereas it was my habit to bake bread once a week, now I had to bake every day, and I came to the conclusion that the reason they sell bread in small province towns "by the yard"— meaning a double loaf about twenty inches long, fourteen inches wide and ten inches high, crusty, stale and never wrapped—is to economize on bread: If it is tasteless, chewy and hard as nails, they won't eat so much.

The boarders were never in the way, they never spoke unless they were spoken to, and they never grumbled. I objected when I caught them spitting on my waxed floor, but I kept my temper and told them politely that I couldn't allow it. They stayed with us three weeks, and I found them to be sincere, obliging and courteous.

Curly often drove to St. Pamphile to the dog kennels to talk with Camille. I never knew anyone quite like Camille. He was a French Canadian, short, wiry and bursting with vitality. He never walked when he could run, and he was constantly on the jump, chattering volubly—half English and half French. The fellow that Camille learned his English from was an expert in profanity—Camille became no less so.

"Jees Crise, Curlee, dat damned dog she's not hugly. De busted ting he's eat Fred Mullen's pants. Crise hi laff. Fred Mullen she run like hell. Got no pant behind!"

When Camille fed the dogs, he bounced—bounced from one kennel to the other, picking up dog dishes, bounced into the storehouse to fill them with mash, and bounced out again to distribute them. Curly says he is a "jumpin' Frenchman."

Chapter 22

St. Pamphile vs. Tourville

C amille was the catcher for the St. Pamphile baseball team, and he and Curly practiced in the cow pasture. "Curlee," he shouted, "you pitch for our team?"

"Gosh no, Camille, I haven't pitched a game for ten years. I'm out of practice."

"Hell, Curlee. Dem damn fools won't know dat. We got a league. We play Tourville, St. Damase, St. Jean Port Joli and St. Anne de la Pocitaire. You come hup next Sunday. We play Tourville."

"OK." Curly laughed.

We went to St. Pamphile the next Sunday. Curly was in his dungarees and woolen sweater, and I in slacks, a daring costume to wear in a small Canadian town. The other young ladies in the audience were dressed in fluttery organdy with many points and flounces around the hem. They wore spike heels and large picture hats decorated with artificial fruit and flowers. Some of the men were in their Sunday suits, with matching hats that had colored feathers stuck into the hatbands. A lot of them wore woods clothes, with clean white shirts and gum rubbers.

As for the players themselves, there wasn't much to distinguish between the two teams. The Tourville contestants were a shade better dressed than the St. Pamphile players (a railroad ran through Tourville, which made the town that much wealthier). They wore colored sweaters—maroon or green—which told the world that they owned two sweaters, this gay one and the customary black, dark blue or gray.

The St. Pamphile team, not to be outshined, had two baseball uniforms to its credit. One was owned by the St. Pamphile first baseman and the other by Camille. Camille's greatest ambition has been also to own a pair of spiked shoes.

My youngest brother, Carl, was with us, and we joined the packed crowd in the cow pasture to watch the game. Many of them didn't know that Carl and I understood their language, and some of the comments about us were amusing: Probably don't own any Sunday clothes. Probably hadn't been to church that morning. Suppose they can understand us? Impossible. Americans can't understand French. It must be because they are dumb. Look at the knife the little boy has on his belt. Better not get too close, never can tell what an American will do.

Someone pushed too close to us, and I asked him, in French, not to. Their faces dropped and the circle around us widened ten feet.

The game was on. Tourville came to bat after much argument around home plate. Curly wound up on the pitcher's mound and beaned the first man with a fastball.

It was easy going after that. They all ducked, and one, two, three men were out. The crowd whooped. Someone who spoke English shouted, "You scare 'em! Curlee youscareem!" St. Pamphile was jubilant. Tourville had been much too cocky lately.

It was St. Pamphile's turn to come to bat. Curly knocked one over the fence, and Camille hit a homer. The ball was lost and the game had to wait while someone went into town to buy another baseball. The first baseman had to go along too, because he owned the store.

The visiting team got a lot of heckling. Carl and I didn't add to the general "good fellowship." We sat on the sidelines between third base and home plate and shouted encouragement. *"Elevez tes pattes!"* Carl yelled to a Tourville player who was trying to beat the ball to home. "Lift your feet! You have your grandmother's legs!" The Tourville man stopped and shook his fist at us. We introduced the Bronx cheer.

They were getting madder by the inning, and the game ended in the fourth with the score sixteen to nothing in favor of St. Pamphile. A fight started on second base, and audience and players congregated on the diamond. Coats and collars came off. Mitts, baseball bats and "cow pies" flew—but Tourville was outnumbered. Their first baseman lost his false teeth, and they willingly retreated from the field.

This was just a bit more exciting a game than I had expected. Baseball is so universally American that I used to think the lumberjacks had invented it. When the men came out of the woods after the drive, they spent their summers playing baseball. Curly had played lumberjack baseball at the Tramway on Eagle Lake, when the fire wardens, game wardens, lumberjacks and scalers used to go to Tramway by canoe just for these Sunday games.

From the accounts given by the few spectators at these Tramway gatherings, the games were more thrilling than big-league baseball. Rules and regulations were invented as the game progressed, and may the man with the best fists win! The

Americans who played at Tramway once organized a first-class team and went over into Canada to play some of the range-road teams. George Gruhn, a forestry supervisor who had been tops in college baseball, left an unbroken record in range-road baseball. He hit a home run nearly every time the ball was pitched to him.

The next Sunday, St. Pamphile went to Tourville to play a return game. We went too and brought along reinforcements, a counselor from one of the boy's canoe parties going downriver. We called him Robin Hood because of the heavy, black beard he had grown during the trip.

St. Pamphile went out on the field to toss a few practice balls, and it was soon evident that Robin Hood could throw a wicked curve. Tourville was reluctant to play. They said the sun would get in their eyes, that their pitcher had a sore arm—that he was helping his wife do the laundry and had caught it in the wringer. They didn't want *le barbu*—the bearded one—to play.

St. Pamphile agreed. They brandished their baseball bats, ready for a scrap, and Tourville weakly excused themselves again. Their first baseman hadn't found his something or other. The St. Pamphile team went back to St. Pamphile and visited the first baseman's wine cellar. Porter and beer make a very good mixture, and mild too.

St. Pamphile won the league pennant that year, and Curly and I were forgiven for our originality in choice of clothing.

Chapter 23

Province of Quebec

We traveled a lot through the Province of Quebec and always enjoyed it. I did tire of the long drive over twisting roads that ran inland from the St. Lawrence River to the boundary. The drive along the St. Lawrence was picturesque, and I was quite astounded the first time I saw one of those little white buildings on the side of the road with the sign CHALET DE NÉCESSITÉ. The villages are identical, with massive churches on the top of a hill. Main Street is a tarred road through the town. Small two-storied houses are unpainted and are built with the clapboards put on vertically. It is said that a painted house in this section means that the owner has worked in the States, and is therefore extravagant.

The church is the center of life, and the better homes, general stores, hotel, filling stations and school gather close to the gray-stone or brick or—very rarely—wooden edifice. Whenever we stopped at a small hotel or a café for lunch, I went through the usual question-and-answer game.

"Where do you come from?" the proprietress asked.

"We come from the States."

"I don't suppose you live in Canada," she continued. "Where are you going?"

"No. We are going home."

"Where do you live?"

"In Maine, on the La Croix road near Lac Frontiere."

She had heard about this road, and she asked more questions before coming to one that really puzzled her. "What kind of an officer is your brother?"

"This isn't my brother. This is my husband. He is a *garde de chasse.*"

She wasn't the least bit abashed. "But he must make a lot of money. You are rich then?"

How often I have heard that question. All French Canadians believe that Americans are millionaires. I laughed. "Yes, we are rich. We are healthy and we live the way we want to live."

"Ah, yes," she sighed. "It is nice to have money."

I thought of our last fifty cents in Curly's pocket, which was to pay for these sandwiches.

Most of the towns in the province are named for saints: St. Prosper, St. Rose, St. Germaine, St. Sabine, St. Camille, St. Justine, St. Georges, St. Marcel, St. Alexandre, St. Helene. There are signs along the road indicating bad turns, crooked hills, winding roads and sharp ascents or descents. The black right angle on the white road sign means a right angle, as we soon discovered when we almost joined the cattle grazing over the fence at the tourists.

Printed signs are in both French and English. *Pont étroit* means a narrow bridge, usually a covered bridge. A friend of ours, while riding through Canada with us, once made the remark, "That must be a big school in Canada, that École School. I wonder when we are coming to it."

The majority of the roads are gravel roads, and they are dusty and washboardy where the top gravel has been washed away. The chief industries are farming and dairying, and some towns can boast of a creamery. The section is not a rich one. The soil is rocky and hilly, and what is not cultivated is freshly burnt and in the process of being cleared for farmland. It is not as scenic as Maine, but it is interesting in its novelty. We were quite startled when we first saw a horse and an ox harnessed together to a high two-wheeled cart.

The roadside shrines are fascinating. Some are just plain crosses, others are a carved figure of Christ on a cross, and a few are small, glassed-in cases that hold a statue of the Virgin. Occasionally on the foot of a shrine there would be a bouquet of limp wild flowers that some child had picked.

Eight miles from St. Pamphile there is one such shrine with a Christ on a cross. Above the cross is a glassed-in case, but the case is empty. There is a story that goes with that empty case with which everyone in the country is familiar.

It seems that in Bill McRea's younger days he drove a certain schoolteacher from Daaquam to St. Pamphile in a sled. But before he was able to reach his destination, a blinding snowstorm came into progress. When he came to the roadside shrine outside of St. Pamphile, he noticed the kerosene lantern that was always placed in the glass case above the carved figure. It seemed to him quite natural to appropriate the lantern so the horse could see the snowdrifts before plowing into them.

When Bill arrived in St. Pamphile he mentioned the fact that he had borrowed this so convenient lantern. The townspeople were outraged. They wanted to tar and feather him.

"Leapin' lizards!" Bill protested, "I had eight more miles to go, and that statue wasn't going anywheres!"

For some reason, the lantern was never replaced in the shrine.

Though we were in the midst of the backwoods, Quebec City was only eighty miles from Nine Mile, directly across the Province of Quebec, over the range roads. A hundred and sixty miles by car in the summertime seemed like a very short drive to us, and on special occasions we would drive to Quebec City for a dance at the Château Frontenac. It was quite a change from Hotel Poulin at Lac Frontiere. The first time we made this trip we left Quebec at two o'clock in the morning and lost ourselves on the bewildering maze of roads and crossroads. We were tired and sleepy, and we drove on endlessly, stopping to look at signs and wishing we had a road map.

"What's this town?" Curly stopped the car and turned a flashlight on the road sign.

"That's just another École School."

It was four o'clock in the morning, and we drove for another hour. "Better take this road," I said. "It seems to be better than the one we are on."

We drove over the road and it ended in a barnyard. We drove back. "Now, which road do we take?" Curly groaned.

"There's the North Star; let's take the other road."

We came to an intersection of roads, with a filling station on one corner. "Now," Curly stated flatly, "I'm going to wake up the guy that lives here and ask him which is the road to Lac Frontiere. Whoever invented this place should have been in a nut house. Hey!" he shouted, pressing on the car horn. "Haloooooo-a! If that doesn't raise him from the dead, nothing will."

A window opened and a man's head appeared. He was sputtering in French.

"Which is the road to Lac Frontiere?" I asked.

"Hunh?" he grunted.

Either he couldn't understand my French, or I couldn't understand his. I repeated the question and always drew a "hunh."

"He's deaf," Curly said. "I'll find out." He stepped out of the car and stood in the middle of the crossing, with one arm pointing toward one of the roads. "Lac Frontiere?" he shouted.

The man shook his head. Curly pointed to all the roads and apparently Lac Frontiere wasn't anywhere. "Quebec?" Curly shouted.

The man nodded, and we discovered that all the roads led to Quebec. We thanked him profusely. Curly got back into the car and we held a consultation. "We'd be better off if we traveled by compass," I suggested.

"You're right. We'll head south."

Daylight found us in another small village on the Maine boundary. We were on the way home at last, after touring the Province of Quebec all night.

On our first trips along the St. Lawrence River, we stopped at every fish wharf and woodcarver's hut along the way. The prices marked on the little wooden figurines were far beyond our means, but we could at least look at them. While indulging in this pastime at one woodcarver's hut, the clerk interrupted us by asking Curly if he was a *garde de chasse* from Maine.

"Yes, I am," Curly said.

The clerk grinned broadly. "Hi know feller *garde de chasse* dere. She's live on La Croix road."

"Is that so?" Curly became all attention. "What's his name?"

"His name is Curlee. Hi know her good. Hi go dere wid Joe Blanchette to go fish."

We didn't have the heart to disillusion him.

179

Chapter 24

Woods Queer

Summer was passing; the nights were growing colder and the mornings were frosty. We caught our last mess of trout at the mouth of Sebemsicook Stream. Summer goes too fast. We have a flash of spring, a cloud of black flies, a few sultry days, and then the air is cool again. More blankets are added to the beds, and we keep a fire burning in the box stove.

We had a beautiful fall season but a twenty-inch snowstorm in October surprised everyone. There were many hunters at Churchill who were unused to driving on snow, and they were feverishly impatient to get out before more snow fell. They were caught between Nine Mile and Clayton, and were all day shoveling out the snow. Frantic hunters walked to Nine Mile.

"May we use your telephone, Mrs. Hamlin?" they inquired.

"Surely."

"What garage in Canada can we call that isn't too far away?"

"You can't call anywhere in Canada," I said.

"What! We can't? What will we do? Who can we call?"

"The nearest central is at the mouth of the Allagash," I explained. "But a call has to be relayed. It is two hundred miles from Fort Kent to here by car."

"We've got to get out of here somehow," they said.

Curly started pulling on his parka. "I can do a little shoveling," he offered. "How many cars are there?"

"Seven, and not one of us can move an inch."

By late afternoon five of the cars had been started on their way, and the other two were shoveled out the next morning.

We always had car trouble in that country. The road was so rough that tires didn't last long, and something was always broken or jarred loose. Car springs didn't last at all, and the nearest place to get them without having to pay a fortune to the Canadian garages was in Fort Kent. Curly once used a yellow birch log for a car spring and drove to Fort Kent with it two months later. It was rough riding but it worked.

Deep snow is difficult to drive on. If a dual-wheeled truck has gone over the road it is impossible to stay on the rut. Car tracks build up, are packed hard by much traveling and then it is equally impossible to stay on the ruts, which are then hardened ridges in the surrounding soft snow.

Curly kept chains on the car. They were old ones that he repaired with telephone wire. A roll of wire was kept behind the seat all the time, and a pair of pliers was in the compartment. When a broken link clanked on the mudguard, he stopped and stepped out of the car.

"Pass me that roll of wire, will you? God bless the Forestry Service. We'd never get anywhere without telephone wire."

"Those chains must be all wire now, aren't they?" I asked.

"Damn near it. When I get new ones I'm going to celebrate. I'm going to drive up and down this road all day, just for the sake of not getting out to fix a link!"

We made two hurried trips downriver for winter groceries, coming back both times with the coupé so heavily loaded that

the body rested on the frame. We drove carefully, looked hopefully at each other after every bump in the road, and stopped
frequently to inspect tires, wishing the roads weren't so icy.

We doubled our grocery list of the year before and added an
equally long list of such items as bitter chocolate, popcorn, wal-
nuts, shredded coconut, dates, marshmallow fluff, sweetened
condensed milk, powdered sugar, cake decorations, fruit juices,
gelatin, pickles, ice-cream mixtures, pie mixtures, canned
pumpkin, oysters, clams, tuna fish, crab meat, Vienna sausages,
sardines, cheddar cheese, tapioca and sharp meat sauces.

Curly was always hungry and was always in the cellar looking for something to eat.

"Where are the Vienna sausages?" he would shout.

"In the second case from the bottom in the third row from
the left."

"Third case in the second row. They're not here! This is
asparagus. Guess I'll try some. I can't find the sausages!"

"Wait a minute, I'll get them. Here."

"What's that?" He'd found something else.

"Shredded coconut."

"Let's try some, and where's that funny-tasting cheese?"

"In the earthen crock."

"You bring it up, my hands are full. Can we eat these pickles now or do we have to wait until February?" He was quite
wild eyed by this time.

"Are you going to eat all that?"

"Oh, sure. I just wanted a lunch before going to bed."

We discovered that mixing the cheddar with a little
Worcestershire sauce made it taste like Roquefort.

I had made green tomato and mustard pickles that fall and
had canned half a pig. We packed forty dozen eggs in earthen

183

crocks, in a solution of water glass—sodium silicate made by fusing together soda ash and clear sand under strong heat. It looks like glass when it is opened in the can, but it is soluble in water, somewhat like a gelatin. Eggs keep very well in it, and I have kept some for a year. The yolks faded and the whites wouldn't whip, but they were still good.

We shot our deer in November and I filled a five-gallon crock with mincemeat. We never could eat that much, and everyone that called at the camp was presented with a quart of mincemeat. This winter we were going to eat if nothing else, and wouldn't be reduced to beans again.

One bright moonlit night, Curly awakened. "Listen, can you hear them?"

I rubbed the sleep out of my eyes. "What is it?"

"Geese, going south."

We heard a faint honking that seemed far, far away. "Let's go outside," I suggested. "Maybe we can see them."

We tumbled out of bed and went out on the lawn. The geese were clearly silhouetted against the November moon—the "mad moon," when birds migrate and even partridges go crazy. It was the first time I had ever seen them, but oh, how they made me want to go with them.

The incident left us with a feeling of loneliness and we couldn't go back to sleep. We put more wood on the dying fire, boiled a kettle of water for hot cocoa, and talked.

One would think that two people would wear out all possible topics of conversation, but we never seemed to. We have different opinions about everything, and we always ended with a hot argument on Frenchmen versus Sons of Ireland. My quarter French and Curly's quarter Irish made the debates slanderous, but it did keep us from brooding.

After living in the woods a long time people are apt to lose their common-sense perspective. If one has nothing to do but think, little things become big, out of all proportion to their real value. Some people brood, others get temperamental, and a few actually break under the strain.

The only time I ever saw Curly angry was when he was changing a tire and the jack wouldn't work. He was mad and said lots of things that wouldn't sound well in some places.

I lost my temper often—so often that it didn't make any impression. If Curly wasn't there to sit down to his meals when they were ready, I slammed the dishes, slammed the cupboard doors, kicked the wood box, hurt my big toe and forgot all about being mad.

Confirmed hermits are really woods queer. They are fussy about their housekeeping. Everything must be exactly where they want it, and they will spend hours straightening dishes on the table or arranging the wood in the wood box. Some talk to themselves, and all of them believe that anything other people do is not done right.

Bill Gordon is an old man who lives at Knowles Brook, about thirty miles above us. He lives all alone in a little cabin and traps—enough to say that he is a trapper. He raises a few potatoes and buys salt pork. He has no cookstove and fries potatoes on the oil-barrel stove. He is a crack shot with a revolver and makes his own ammunition. He doesn't like to have people call on him, and he doesn't like to come to "civilization"— meaning Nine Mile—to get his mail. He won't hunt because he has made pets of all the animals around his camp and even has a pool of pet trout. He doesn't have a radio or a telephone, and no one knows what he actually does with his time.

We see him twice a year, once in the spring, and once in the fall when he comes down the river in his canoe to get his mail. His long white hair hangs to his shoulders and two heavy guns and cartridge belts are strapped to his waist. There is always a heavy package for him containing materials for more cartridges. One year he had a registered letter telling him to come to Fort Kent and get some money that the bank owed him. He wouldn't go. Said they could keep it. He'd be damned if he'd ride on a train.

One fall when Bill came down I had a bottle of wine that a fisherman priest had left us. I treated Bill to a water glass of wine and he gulped it. I filled it up twice more and Bill opened up and talked. Nothing was right. Why did they build the bridge at Nine Mile? If they hadn't done that there wouldn't be so many people around. Automobiles were instruments of the Devil. The radio was a defiance of God. The whole damned shebang was going to pot. He couldn't get a haircut. He wouldn't go to Daaquam for a haircut if they paid him to.

"I'll cut your hair, Bill," I offered.

"All right, but be sure you cut it right. I don't want none of them fancy haircuts. Just straight all around!"

After his haircut, Bill went back to Knowles Brook to hibernate through another winter.

Chapter 25

Dogs

Our experiences of the previous winter had taught us much, and we decided to train a team of dogs to use during the winter. That spring at Umsaskis, Boots had had nine black cuddly puppies. We found them squirming and squeaking under the porch steps one early June morning. Five females and one male died of distemper, and we kept the other two males, Beer and Pretzel, and gave Isobelle to Pete Pellerin at Long Lake dam.

They resembled German shepherds—police dogs—but Pretzel showed the strong husky strain of his forefathers. It was some time before we could decide that Boots had to go. Contrary to popular belief, a female dog is not an asset to a team. I put it off as long as possible, but one day Curly brought up the subject.

"We'll have to go after that lead dog soon so we'll get a chance to know him."

I was standing by the window, and I didn't turn around. "I know, and Boots will have to go."

We took her to Monk, Canada, loaded her into a crate and shipped her back to my home in Fort Kent. She would be royally welcomed by the neighborhood children.

Beer, one of the pups, was grayish black around the chest and legs, with a black saddle and a masked face. Pretzel was unfriendly, but he was the more faithful of the two dogs. He was lighter in color and had a longer and silkier fur.

They were inseparable and playful—so playful that when they were only five months old they ate a hindquarter of a deer that we had hanging in the shed, and for days they lay on the porch, bloated and happy. We let them run loose in the yard and watched them constantly, driving them back from the road with a light switch. Rapping on the windowpane would sometimes turn them back when they planned to chase a car, and by fall they couldn't be coaxed out of the dooryard.

We visited the private kennels in St. Pamphile where they raised huskies for racing in Quebec. Usually these dogs were not for sale, but we bought a Siberian husky, a leader that had been discarded in favor of the faster, mongrel type of dog. The other husky teammates had been killed, but the leader was kept for Curly.

Loupe (French for wolf) was pure white and slant eyed. He had a snobbish expression, but he was a wise old trail dog, knowing no other god than his master. We didn't know how old he was because he had been brought into the country on an ice-breaker from the north four years previously. He was a veteran in a harness, had a nasty disposition, an intelligence better than average, and was a natural-born leader.

The kennel owner had had him four years, and the first year Loupe won the Quebec dogsled races. The last two years Loupe hadn't been off his chain. He was quite ragged looking, but after worming him we had a new dog. His coat became soft, shiny and silky, and he walked proudly with short stubby ears erect and tail curled on his back. He snapped and snarled at any discipline, but Curly soon took him down a few pegs with mittened fists—never sticks or boots.

The first night Loupe stayed with us, we kept him in a wire-enclosed kennel. He was gone in the morning and I frantically called everyone in the country to be on the lookout for him. We jumped into the car and drove to Clayton, thinking he might be along the road. On our way back to camp as we were crossing the bridge, we saw him sitting under the riverbank, absorbed in watching the river.

Loupe inspected the inside of the camp cautiously, slinking like a wolf in captivity and backing off with hackles raised when one of us moved. He could jump square footed over the table, and he delighted in showing off. Curly would make him jump through the little opening over the sideboard and into the living room, and when I had coached Curly in French—*venez ici*, come here, and *couche toi*, lie down—he and Loupe could carry on a conversation. It was shortened to *viens* and *couche*. *Viens* meant anything to Loupe: come here, quiet, turn around, get up; and *couche* meant lie down, sit down, get on the bench, or scram!

Two weeks later Curly came home with another new dog. "What is it?" I asked. "An ox?"

"That's our new dog!"

"Where did you get anything that size?"

"St. Pamphile. Nice, isn't he?" Curly staggered when the dog playfully leaped on him.

"Has it got a name?" I dodged it.

"It isn't an it, it's a he. His name is Poo."

"Now look," I protested, "you're not going to name any dogs after me."

"I'm not kidding, his name is really Poo. But maybe we'd better call him Poo-Poo."

Poo-Poo's heart was bigger than he was, and a more faithful and better-dispositioned dog wasn't to be found anywhere. We loved him, scolded him and petted him, but we couldn't punish him. He meant well, and if his prancing bowled us over and his claws ripped our clothes, he couldn't be blamed for it.

Poo-Poo was short haired and black with a bearlike head. He was as big as a Great Dane, playful, comic and awkward, a rowdy and a roughneck. Unlike most dogs, Poo-Poo didn't mind being a clown. He was bred in St. Pamphile for racing and he was strong, wiry and fast.

We never could stop him from howling at the moon, and those cold, silvery nights were twice as mournful with Poo-Poo serenading us. He made the other dogs restless at such times, and all night we could hear them pacing back and forth with their chains rattling nervously.

Once when Poo-Poo had been with us for only a short while, I went to his kennel to let him off his chain. Thinking he might run away, I grasped his collar firmly and started for the camp. In a split second we unexpectedly landed on the doorstep. Poo-Poo was still on his feet, but I wasn't. Curly had the same experience, and we learned to lift him off his front feet by the collar, so he wouldn't get such a toehold.

It was great fun to send visitors to unhook Poo-Poo, warning them to hold his collar lest he run away. The results were always the same, and even Poo-Poo caught the spirit of the game and no one could hold him. We kept him tied with the same type of chain that we used on the other dogs, but after he broke two of them and rammed out the side of his kennel, we used a heavier chain.

Poo-Poo's one desire when he was loose was to come into the camp. He would race down the knoll on a dead run, ram his head on the door and nearly take it off the hinges, all in fun. Once he was in the camp he bumped into everything, skidded on the linoleum, juggled the box stove and shook down the soot. He moved over under the table and stood up to stretch. The table legs were lifted off the floor, the bowl of apples upset, and Poo-Poo was in chase after them.

Curly talked "dogs" morning, noon and night. He was delighted when anyone stopped to see the dogs, and glowing with pride, he escorted them from kennel to kennel.

"Now this one is my leader, a Siberian husky. I don't know how old he is, but he must be nearly ten. *Viens*, Loupe. He won't bite." (A menacing growl from Loupe with hackles raised and teeth bared. The visitors retreated.) "*Couche*, Loupe. He won't bite, not when I'm here anyway. These are the two pups I raised myself, husky and police. Down, Beer! Down, Pretzel! Yes, quite heavy chested. Notice the dewclaws on Beer. I keep Poo-Poo back of the camp. He's big all right, but he wouldn't hurt a kitten. Why don't you unhook him and bring him down? Be sure you hang onto his collar so he won't run away."

The dog food problem was solved when Joe Deblois called us on the phone one day.

"Do you want some dog meat?" he asked.

"You bet we do," I said.

"My horse fell over the bank and broke its back, and I had to shoot him."

"We'll be right up, Joe, and thanks loads. A whole horse?" I added, quite elated at the prospects.

Joe laughed. "Yes, a whole horse."

I hung up. "Come on, Curly. Joe has a whole horse we can have!"

"Is it dead?" he asked.

I think we were both a bit stupefied.

It was unquestionably dead. We quartered it and brought it back to Nine Mile, and Curly cut it into two-pound pieces, a daily ration for each dog. It froze and kept during the winter, and had to be thawed behind the kitchen stove before being fed to the dogs. We bought a thousand pounds of dog mash, out of which I made dog bread—really a process of mixing the mash with water, sometimes adding flour, baking powder and salt and baking it in large sheets. The aroma around the kitchen at such "dog bread baking rallies" was indelicate to say the least. Mixing it was like making mudpies, with sleeves rolled and arms deep in grayish paste. It took hours to bake, and I couldn't put anything else in the oven because of the strong, fishy old meat smell.

The dogs were fed once a day. If we forgot them, in the late afternoon a chorus started outside. Loupe howled, Beer rumbled, Pretzel yip-yipped, and Poo-Poo took the high notes like a prima donna. It was more agonizing than a barbershop quartet. Curly fed them, but when he wasn't home, I ran out to the garage, grabbed a two-pound piece of horse meat and a loaf of dry bread for each dish, ran to each kennel distributing the dishes, and ran back into the warm camp, breathless in the sudden silence that reigned.

During the summer when the dogs were loafing, rations were reduced. They had just a loaf of bread and sometimes the chub we caught in the river. There were thousands of chub in front of the camp, and we stood on the bridge, let the line drop with a piece of worm or salt pork, and hauled them in hand over hand.

Each dog was chained separately and the chains were looped on fifty-foot wires, allowing plenty of freedom of movement.

The dogs didn't mind being tied up. Loupe had never known anything else, and the pups had been tied from the time they were six months old. They fought it like mad in the beginning, biting and yanking at the chain, and getting twisted in it until they learned to make large circles and unwind themselves from a tree trunk. When they were loose in the yard, and we said "Go to your house!" they went, and stayed until we hooked the chain to their collars again. The pups had kennels on the porch of the schoolhouse, with wires to the riverbank. Loupe's kennel was on the riverbank with his wire stretching to the guest cabin. The pups couldn't be reached without passing Loupe, and a lot of people wouldn't risk that. He hated strangers, and when one approached he growled and jumped against his chain, mostly bluffing, although there were days when he was ill tempered. There were always some who were foolish enough to think we didn't know our own dogs and they would be quite frightened when Loupe's snarling leap brought him too close for comfort.

Of course the dogs had their exercise, working in the sled in the wintertime, which they loved, and in the summertime running and wrestling on the lawn before a daily swim with us. Beer and Pretzel raced like greyhounds chasing each other's tails, dodging the trees, pounding over the porch and wheeling on their hind legs to tumble all over the lawn. They were big dogs, weighing about seventy pounds each, and it was amusing to watch them prance on their hind feet, clinched like boxers, throwing each other and running again, Beer's plumed tail tightly grasped in Pretzel's jaws. Loupe was a lone wolf and snobbishly retreated from such prankish insults.

In the water the pups were like two children, dashing in, pawing out to the rock in the middle of our swimming hole, climbing up with us and diving off, yelping and splashing.

Loupe hated the water and was wild when anyone else went in. He followed us around, swimming and struggling, trying to head us toward the shore or onto the rock. If strangers went in he grabbed them by the arm and tried to pull them out. When we hung onto his tail he would tow us in, making little whimpering noises. Poo-Poo absolutely refused to go in the water, but he raced up and down the bank, cheering us on.

Swimming was our relief from the black flies. They couldn't get us underwater, but the moose flies—big, fat, black-and-yellow-striped flies that weren't satisfied with simple bites—nearly drove us crazy. Black flies bothered the pups and we kept sulphur and lard on their sore, bloody ears. Loupe's fur was thick and kept the flies out, but they dug in around his eyes and we had constantly to keep watch and brush them off.

Had we let the dogs run loose, they would have chased everything in the woods. Loupe was a well-known killer, having killed nine sheep and three cows in an hour's escape from his last kennel. A deer wouldn't have had a chance with the two pups. But the greatest danger was from porcupines. A dog does not know the bear's tactics in killing a porcupine, turning it over and leaving the belly exposed. A dog will charge and get a mouthful of quills.

We once lost a beautiful, long-haired Labrador husky that had tried to eat a porcupine. His head, mouth and throat were plastered with quills. Curly had no ether or chloroform at Umsaskis, and after chaining the dog with his back to a tree, wedging his jaw open with a piece of wood and trying vainly to pull out the quills against ninety pounds of raging, insanely struggling dog, he finally had to shoot him. That incident made a strong impression on us, made me feel that it is criminal to allow a dog to run loose in the woods.

I dislike porcupines. They are supposedly harmless creatures, the quills their only protection against a ruthless nature. But actually they are very destructive. They gnaw and chew wood-work, furniture, canoes, paddles, snowshoes—anything in a camp that is left uninhabited for a time. We have removed many quills from dogs. We would tie the dog or hold him, and pull out each quill with pliers—a quick jerk directly in line with the slant of the quill. Curly once had a cocker spaniel that was always coming home with his nose bristling with porcupine quills; and he was so used to having them pulled out, he lay quietly while it was done, only whimpering a little.

Boots was the only dog I ever knew who could kill a porcu-pine and emerge unscathed. She turned it on its back, the way a bear does, and devoured the whole carcass, getting only one or two quills in her nose. After our experience with Bergan, the Labrador, we kept a can of ether at the camp, but never had occasion to use it because we kept our dogs tied.

Loupe received the most attention because he was expected to keep the other dogs in line. He was so class-conscious with the pups that he wouldn't allow them to run by him or go through the door before he did. It was amusing to watch him strut up to the screen door, leisurely taking his time, with the two pups nudging and shoving behind him but not daring to hurry him too much. "Look at him," Curly said. "If that isn't a smirk on a dog's face, I never saw one."

Curly fed him the scraps from the table, or what was left when I was through feeling sorry for Poo-Poo and the pups and had selected the biggest bones for them. I spent a lot of spare time at their kennels, sometimes feeding them or letting them hunt for scraps in the pockets of my mackinaw. They coaxed with sad, brown eyes, nudging the bulging pocket, and poked their noses down cautiously to pull out a fish head or a piece of dry toast.

Loupe was Curly's dog and was quite obviously unaware of such an insignificant person as myself. He obeyed me because he had to. If I were sweeping he followed the broom around with his nose to the floor, sniffing for crumbs. One day, in an uncalled-for flare of annoyance, I brushed him aside with the broom. Before I could shout, Loupe had grabbed the broom from my hands, held my wrist clenched between his teeth and was staring me in the eye.

I never moved a muscle, but perspiration oozed out all over me. I called softly to Curly in the next room. "Better come out here, but don't startle the dog."

When Loupe saw Curly coming into the room, he let go of my wrist. Curly threw him outside, pummeled him in the snow, and chained him to his kennel.

For two days no one spoke to Loupe, but when I fed him he looked so ashamed and brokenhearted, I relented and brought him back into the fold. That was the last time he ever showed antagonism toward anyone in the camp.

He obeyed the snap of a finger. He never snatched at food that was offered to him, but took it gingerly between his teeth, laid it down and looked up for permission to eat it. If he stole a piece of thawing horse meat from behind the stove, I took it away from him and he gave me that "Well, well, how did that get here?" expression.

Chapter 26
A Dog's Life at Nine Mile

We bought a twelve-foot racing sled built entirely of ash, except for the steel-shod runners that extended about five feet behind the upright handlebars. The sled was strong and wiry, and the driver could slew the sled around by leaning on one runner. We spliced ropes around the base of the back uprights, centering the strain on the sled, and around the front braces to keep the traces from spreading or falling back. Curly could splice the best loops, but I did the splicing that joined two loose ends, and between us and a coat of shellac, the sled shone like a frosty morning.

It was just the right size for four dogs. Two people could ride in it, although the seat was uncomfortable and the extra weight on the front of it made it travel harder in deep snow. Most of the time the seat was packed with Curly's traveling equipment—an ax, snowshoes and a rifle strapped to the side, a sleeping bag and air mattress rolled into a duffel bag, a knapsack with food, extra socks, cartridges and matches, and a bag of dog rations—loaves of bread and pieces of frozen meat.

We also bought a twelve-foot dog whip, not for our dogs but for the Canadian mutts along the border. A dog team will

197

collect dogs of every description in the country, but once the whip is uncoiled and cracked over them, they disappear like magic.

When the whip came, I took it out on the lawn, swirled it in real teamster fashion and lashed forth in what was meant to be a crack like a rifle shot. It didn't crack but it darn near took my ears off when it wrapped itself around my neck.

Training sled dogs requires a lot of patience and stubbornness, and Curly had both. The pups were five months old when we put them in a harness and, one at a time, hooked them to the single sled and tried to make them follow us. It didn't work.

Curly decided to go into it wholeheartedly. We harnessed the four dogs to the sled—Loupe first, Pretzel next, then Beer, and last of all, Poo-Poo "on the pole," the position next to the sled and the toughest. The last dog takes all the punishment on curves. When a long team of dogs swings sharply, the last dog is lifted bodily if he can't hold his own. He also gets the bumps if a driver isn't careful.

Reluctant dogs that show stubbornness can be easily cured by putting them "on the pole" and urging them with the bow of the sled. Loupe was humiliated whenever he was on the pole, but it took the cussedness out of him. Poo-Poo didn't mind the disgrace. It was all one with him.

Curly and I had all we could do to harness them, but we couldn't hold them, and we were both dragged a hundred yards before they were stopped. We shouted, our clothes were torn and our faces and arms were scratched. We tied a rope on Poo-Poo's harness and anchored him to a two-foot butt of a pine tree in the dooryard.

Loupe bounced like a rubber ball, barking at us and leaping forward. The pups strained to get out of their harnesses. Poo-Poo

lunged forward and was stopped sharply by the rope. As soon as
one dog was quieted—by talking to him, scratching his ears or
administering a cuff with a leather mitten—another started and
the whole chorus joined in.

"Why don't you let them run it off?" I suggested, hanging
to Loupe's collar with my feet digging into the ground.

"They know better than that. They know that I want them
to lie down, and they're going to do it."

"Poo-Poo is causing all the trouble. He doesn't know what
we want him to do."

"Maybe, but he might as well learn now."

Again Poo-Poo lunged against the rope, squawking when it
choked him.

Two hours later they were subdued to an occasional whim-
per. Curly stood on the runners and I unhooked Poo-Poo. They
tore over the knoll behind the camp. Loupe was digging for all
he was worth, dragging the pups. Gravel and snow flew, and
Curly claims the sparks rolled out from under them. Beer and
Pretzel decided to get up and run when Loupe snarled at them,
and the team was off down the road, lickety-split.

I followed with the car and we spent the rest of the day
teaching Poo-Poo not to get ahead of the other dogs. He had
been in a harness before and had been trained with a team of
racing dogs. He had been taught to go the minute he wasn't
held, and at the kennels in St. Pamphile it required eight men
to harness eight dogs. We would have difficulty finding even
four people at Nine Mile to harness four dogs whenever Curly
wanted to use them.

The next few days the pups were less bewildered and they
were as anxious to go as Loupe and Poo-Poo were. Every day the
rides were longer and the dogs were learning to pull harder and

faster. The hard work of training came when they had to be taught to lie still in their harnesses, never moving until they heard the command "All right!" For a while we had to hold them all the time. Later we didn't have to hold them, but the moment Curly put his foot on the runners they started. It was two more weeks before they could be broken of that habit.

He trained them to wait on the trail, lying in their harnesses and never moving while he left them. It was a proud Mr. Hamlin who came back to camp one day and announced that he'd "done it."

"Done what?" I asked absentmindedly.

"Woman! What do you think I've been doing this past month?" He poured a pint of syrup over a mound of two dozen corn fritters. "Why, I have the dogs trained so I can leave them anywhere, and they won't move until I call them."

"Really!" This was the tone I should have used in the first place.

We had a first-rate dog team, but the credit goes to Curly. He fed them, petted them, punished them and disciplined them, and drove them anywhere and everywhere. The dogs would have walked the pads off their feet for him, and Loupe would still be pulling when the trail was long and the pups were tired. After six weeks of steady training, the four dogs could easily do thirty and forty miles in a day, and after three months of training they have done fifty and even sixty miles in one day.

After a short excursion one morning, Curly came back to camp with a torn parka, broken dog harnesses and a crestfallen leader. The ash bow on the front of the sled was smashed.

"Whatever have you been through?" I asked. "A keg of nails?"

"Might just as well have been," he said. "Loupe spotted the trapper's cat and decided he wanted it."

"One tabby cat didn't cause all that trouble."

"You'd be surprised. I couldn't hold the whole team and if we hadn't run into a tree, we'd still be larrupin' through a cedar swamp. I'll bet that white devil doesn't chase any more cats." He ruefully inspected the damage to the sled and harnesses. "I have an iron rod in the shed that will just fit this, but I need different harnesses. How much money have we?"

This dog team business was expensive, there was no getting around it.

The dog harnesses we had were the ordinary light webbing that is used in the north because dogs will eat leather. They had been made for racing purposes, and were much too light for the type of work Curly wanted them for. We bought padded dog collars, strips of tough leather, boxes of rivets, shoemaker's needles, waxed thread, buckles, rings and snaps from a mail-order catalogue.

Curly worked a week and a half to make three harnesses, using the living room as a workshop. He cut, sewed, riveted, and fitted each dog separately. The floor was littered with scraps of leather, bent rivets and dogs, and I had to ask permission to wade through the living room.

"Look out!" he yelled. "You're stepping on my traces!"

"I only wanted to go to the bedroom."

"Holy Moses, you've been there forty times today. Come here and hold this for me, will you?"

I had almost reached the bedroom but I turned and waded back. "So that's where my nail scissors went to!"

"Your what! Oh, these things. Are they nail scissors? I thought they were to cut round holes with."

"I've been looking all over the place for them. You're going to ruin them!"

"Now, Pooie," he protested, jabbing another hole in the leather, "you know these are just the thing to cut round holes with."

When he was done he had three perfect leather harnesses that would never tangle or break. We hoped that after all the trouble of cutting horse meat, the harnesses wouldn't be eaten too. Besides, they cost me one pair of nail scissors.

Whenever I drove the dogs I had trouble with Loupe. He knew more about it than I did, and turned quickly and started back to camp. I jumped off the runners, grabbed him as he went by and cuffed him with the mittens while he stuck his head in the snow and growled, watching me out of the corner of his eye to see if I were frightened.

I like to ride a dogsled. It is like skiing, balancing on the runners, steering with the feet, using the handlebars to keep the sled upright and as an added balance on sharp curves. The dogs ran smoothly, heads even with shoulders, backs slightly sway-ing—unhurried after the first enthusiastic outburst of energy. Each dog was in step, paced by Loupe and leaving a trail that looked as though one dog and a sled had gone over the snow. Loupe kept his tail curled on his back, like a proud knight lead-ing his squires.

They averaged seven or eight miles an hour, but they would pick up speed when spoken to, and a fast ride was accompanied with a chant.

"Come on-n-n, Pretzel! Good ole Pretzel. Come on-n-n, Beer! Atta boy, Beer. Come on-n-n, Louie, you ole fox. Tighten up your traces. Come on-n-n, Poo-Poo! You ole meat eater, you're better than four horses. When it's spring-g-g-time in the Rockies. Come on-n-n, Beer, good ole Beer. I'll be coming-g-g back to you-u-u. Come on-n-n, Pretzel! Come on-n-n, Poo-Poo! Come on-n-n, Louie!"

Mile after mile sped behind me as the dogs raced along, uphill and down, turning sharply on the curves for an exciting skid on frozen snow. Nippy wind reddened cheeks and nose. A flurry of snow from an evergreen dropped on my parka hood and shoulders, and after a ten-mile exercise run, I was home again, exhilarated but with wrist and leg muscles lame.

A dog team once drove into our yard where our two pups were harnessed. Loupe was loose and when he saw the strange leader, he was outraged. He flashed into the team, snapping, biting and slashing. Curly and the driver waded into them with leather moccasins flying, and as soon as one dog was loose I grabbed him and started for the camp. Loupe left a mark on every one of the dogs before Curly finally lifted him from the raging pack, with only a small cut over his eye.

I corralled the other four dogs into the camp where another trapper was sitting with his small pet dog. He shouted for help, standing in the middle of the floor with his dog in his arms and four playful brutes leaping around him to get a sniff.

"*Nom de nom*! *Maudit chiens*! *Venez, Madame Curlee*! Dogs she is want to eat Pepe. Get hout, hi come mad quick. Hi catch you by de face!"

When the snow had packed harder we harnessed the dogs and rode to Lac Frontiere. Everyone in the village wanted a ride in the dog sled, or to drive them. Dog teams are common in the Province of Quebec, but a four-dog team as well-behaved, friendly and fast as ours was like a Pied Piper. It collected its own parade.

We harnessed the dogs, and the girls and women went for the first rides. Loupe and the dogs seemed to know they were on exhibition and they raced like mad up and down Main Street. Snow flew from under their paws and back onto the sled. Loupe's tail was curled tightly on his back and the passengers screamed when the sled skidded on a curve. Several of the boys attempted to drive them, but Curly had to start Loupe himself by shouting "All right!"

Away they went. Within a hundred yards Loupe discovered that Curly wasn't on the sled, and back he came, turning quickly and throwing the drivers. One amusing incident occurred when one of these would-be drivers was swung over the handlebars in a loop to find himself sitting comfortably in the sled. Curly asked him how he did it.

"Me I get hon de runner. *Le chien blanc*, she's not know she's me dere, I tink. Den he's turn. Hi go hup hin de hair. It's me hin de sled. Big surprise!"

Curly started for the mouth of Big Black River one day, and the next afternoon he called me on the telephone. "Hello, Pooie! Guess where I am?"

"I can't imagine, but I hope you haven't been pinched."

"I'm in Fort Kent!"

He had traveled with the dogs to Allagash in a day and a half—a distance of sixty-eight miles. Coming home he made the same time, fifty miles the first day and eighteen miles the next forenoon, but the dogs were as thin as skeletons. Poo-Poo looked more like a greyhound than a sled dog. It was a long trip for them, but the amount of work they can do is surprising.

Chapter 27

Nine Mile Winter

One dark morning there were three suns burning on the horizon—a sign of a heavy storm. Two were sundogs, reflections through the unsettled atmosphere. The river froze over, slushing on cold nights, whispering and quieting as the frost caught it and held. The next day the ice ran in thin sheets. Each day the sheets were thicker and slower to break away, and they sluggishly slowed until they had stopped—jagged, uneven and tightening. The river was silent now. Snow fell, and then more snow.

The mailman couldn't come in, and Christmas rolled around with no prospects of a celebration. I trimmed a small tree with homemade decorations and made candy with the cookie press. Curly went to Lac Frontiere with the dogs to see if he could get our mail from the Canadian post office. When he came back I looked ruefully at the empty sled. "Couldn't get anything?"

"No, but I've got a chicken and a Christmas present for you."

"You have? Let's see it. What is it?"

"Chocolates."

"Um-m-m." I bit into one. "What's the matter with them?"

"They were all Gregoire had, and I think they've been in the store since July."

We sat on the couch with Loupe between us, munching chocolates and feeding them to the dog who coaxed with his cold nose in my neck. We listened to Christmas carols on the radio and really felt Christmasy. The people at Clayton and Churchill were no better off than we were, and I felt sorry for Joe Giguare's children. They didn't have any presents at Christmas time, and it means so much to youngsters.

We didn't need Christmas cards. Every window was a Christmas card, more beautiful than any I ever saw. There was so much snow that it lay five feet deep on the ground. The trees were weighted with it. It clung to the telephone wire and set it swaying with an almost perpetual motion. It piled high on the outside windowsills, and even the bare maples and birches were decked with ermine coats.

We were so busy training the dogs we didn't notice how fast the time went by. I had bought crossword-puzzle books and yarn, and we had a new collection of books. Some thoughtful soul had left two four-foot stacks of old *Life* magazines at our door.

I knitted stockings all winter, sometimes adding new feet to leggings that were hardly worn at all. Whenever Curly went to Lac Frontiere, I had him bring back more yarn. It was seldom the same color, and so some of the stockings were green, red, brown, tan and maroon, whichever color he happened to fancy at the time. Heels and toes were almost always a different color.

Another occupation consisted of the three meals a day I prepared. Curly was up at seven every morning. He built the fires, warmed the camp, played the radio and rattled the spiders on the cookstove. "Come on, get up! I want my breakfast!"

"It didn't take long for you to forget how to fry bacon and eggs."

"No back talk now. Get up! What do you think I married you for?"

"That isn't what you told me!"

I stuck my head out of the top bunk and looked out over the tops of the frosted windowpanes. Coated and shiny trees sparkled in the morning sunlight and snowdrifts reached halfway to the roof of the camp. I ducked back under the blankets, closed my eyes tightly, and tried to shut out the noises of pots and pans rattling.

"I'm coming in with a cup of cold water!" He rattled a dipper against the water pail and I dived out of bed.

From the kitchen windows we could see the dog kennels. Beer and Pretzel were inside theirs with heads showing around the corners, watching the camp and ready to come out and bark good morning. Loupe never slept in his kennel but buried himself in the snow, and the only thing that distinguished him from a snowdrift were three black dots for his eyes and nose.

If I had set bread to rise during the night, I baked it in the morning. Sometimes I baked a pie or a pudding, and put meat in a Dutch oven on the back of the stove, so it would be tender for supper. I have two favorite recipes for the small, tough scraps from the foreshoulders and ribs of a deer. I dredge the meat in flour and salt, braise it in hot fat, add a grated carrot, a grated onion, celery salt and a pint of tomato juice, and allow it to simmer on the back of the stove for six hours. It is tender, has no gamey taste, and the gravy is delicious. The other method of cooking it is an old French Canadian recipe, similar to the first, but in this one only water, small red onions and a finely chopped garlic are added, and it is simmered slowly for twelve hours.

Some meat I cold-packed and canned, but the only meal I could make with it was a deep-dish meat pie. I later precooked venison with onions or green peppers before canning it. There is a definite gamey flavor to deer meat that is noticeable after the first few steaks.

We had half a pig hanging in the guest cabin where we kept everything that could be frozen and preserved, and we had many pork chops, pork steaks and pot roasts with browned potatoes. Sometimes Curly brought in beef steak from Lac Frontiere, but it was so tough I had to simmer it all day in tomato juice before we could eat it.

In the small province towns, meat is all the same price, and all tough. My sister visited us one fall, and on a tour of the Lac Frontiere stores she found a "bargain." Sirloin steak was fourteen cents a pound! She bought five pounds, and when she excitedly called me on the phone to keep supper waiting for the sirloin steak that was only fourteen cents a pound, I told her to take it back and have them make hamburger out of it.

"But this is sirloin, and only fourteen cents a pound!"

"I know," I said. "It's fourteen cents a pound if you get it off the neck too."

She cooked it and discovered it really wasn't worth more than fourteen cents.

Curly wouldn't go to bed unless he'd had his fourth meal of the day. If I thought it was too much effort to make golden toast or flapjacks, I fed him the leftovers from our dinner. If he was still hungry he'd eat four quarts of popcorn. He'd sit on the couch with one of his books and munch popcorn until I thought he'd burst.

I read everything as quickly as possible and was reduced to crossword puzzles during the winter. The nights were noisy, especially when the temperature dropped quickly. The sudden contraction of the steel bridge in cold weather made it vibrate like a highly pitched tuning fork. The camp seemed to vibrate with it. The constant hum is an odd sensation. One never fully loses consciousness of it, as when a clock ticks, and when the temperature dropped to forty and fifty below zero, the humming grew sharper and higher in pitch. It was hard to go to sleep, and the radio didn't drown it out at all.

It was on one such night that I chilled a can of evaporated milk for a few minutes, then whipped it until it was stiff, added a beaten egg, sugar, vanilla and cocoa, and set it outside to freeze. Within fifteen minutes we had ice cream.

There would be half an inch of beautiful, lacy frost on the windowpanes, and a red-hot fire had to be kept burning all night. Forty degrees below zero sounds cold. It is cold—a dry, suffocating cold. The coldest I ever experienced was fifty-four below, when I had to breathe through a woolen scarf. But I would rather see forty below in Aroostook County than ten below near the seacoast where a damp wind cuts through woolen clothes as though they were gauze.

We had good radio reception at Nine Mile. There was no interference, and the coldest nights were the best. "Dance, Curly!" I dragged him off the couch. "Here's your favorite, the Blue Danube."

Chapter 28

Neighbors

That first winter at Nine Mile, we had neighbors across the river. Of the two bachelor trappers that had once lived in the lumber camp, one shot the other through the arm. The culprit had to go to Houlton, and Brooks, the victim who had received only a flesh wound, lived alone until he married a girl from Lac Frontiere.

She couldn't speak English and he couldn't speak French. He trapped for a living and guided during the summer. Hermanse, his wife, was young, but like all French Canadian girls, she had matured early. It was good to have them near. Curly could talk about his dogs to Brooks, and Hermanse could play double solitaire.

I snowshoed over to play cards with Hermanse and she visited at our camp, until Curly frightened her. He bounced in one day, flourishing the bullwhip. "By the Holy Ole Mackinaw! I'm the mayor of Nine Mile and if you women don't scuttle around and get me some grub, I'll plunk you in a snowbank, bottoms up!"

I grabbed a pillow. "You are having delusions, Mr. Hamlin. I am the big frog in this puddle!"

Nine Mile Bridge

The last I saw of Hermanse, she was flying through the door. The next time I saw her she was very sorry that my husband beat me. I agreed, but I didn't tell her she should have stayed around to see who got the biggest mouthful of feathers.

Pillows didn't last long in our family.

Brooks had boarders for a month. Two cruisers were estimating the timberlands for a lumber company, and they stayed at Brooks's camp. Almost every night the population of Nine Mile, six of us, gathered around the long table in our living room with cards and matches for a game of poker, dealer name the game, jacks or better to open and a one-cent limit.

Poker is a fascinating game. Everyone who lives in the woods plays it. It can go on for hours and hours, and if it isn't a cutthroat game it doesn't require the concentrated attention of that bore of all bores—bridge. The lingo that goes with poker is colorful. The terms "deuces and treys" or "nits and lice" for twos and threes are familiar. More confusing are "bulls" for aces, "bitches" for queens, "devil's bedpost" for the four of clubs, "hooks" for sevens and "thirty days" for a ten spot and "Mistrigris," the original name for poker played with a wild card—though I often wonder who invented that one.

Hermanse learned a lot of English during those evenings, both good and indifferent.

"Two cents." Someone bet on a small pair showing.

"Hi got no matches." Hermanse had a queen on the board. "Hi tell to Brooks she lend me, he hask me no. Where I get some?"

"You have a good hand, Hermanse?"

"Sure ting. Hi got a *chienne* hin de hole."

Strangely enough, though these people lived on the same spot on the map as ourselves, they didn't seem real to us. I suppose

we had become too accustomed to being alone. One of the cruisers stayed there only a week, and decided he liked the bright
lights better. The other stayed on, shouldering his pal's work as
well as his own.

We did get to know Adrian and liked him very much. He
had that quiet reserve that I have come to recognize in timber
cruisers. On the few occasions when he would talk, we learned
many surprising things about him. He had worked in the mines
of Abitibi, in Canada, been a bellhop in a Montreal hotel while
going to night school, and trapped mink north of the St.
Lawrence River. He told us that the mink there were larger than
ours but that the fur wasn't as fine. Adrian himself was curious
about everything. At Nine Mile he saw a pileated woodpecker
for the first time in his life, and he was quite impressed by it.

When the time came for Adrian to leave, we really hated to
see him go. He was one of those people who make you feel you
want to know everything about him—and you never will.

Chapter 29

Canine First Aid

Our mail came in February, when Cyril Jandreau borrowed a horse and sled from Narciss and went to Lac Frontiere. He broke a trail for the horse and stayed overnight with us. On his way back the sled was piled high with Christmas packages and we waylaid him again to stay overnight. Most of the packages were outside the mailbags, and several were for us. Some of our gifts were food. Curly opened one package that had been damaged because of its long wait in a post office.

"What is it?" I bent over the mess.

"I think it used to be sweet potatoes, apples and candy."

"Here is something covered with green mold, looks like rye bread." I pulled out a long package, also covered with mold. "Now what in the world is this?"

Curly cut it with a knife. "It's a salami!"

"Do you suppose it's any good?"

"Would be, if we can get the mold off," he said.

I washed it in vinegar and it was as good as new.

Curly went to Clayton to get our two months' collection of letters. The radio wasn't working again, and we packed it to go to Clayton on the dogsled. We also sent the following letter:

Nine Mile Bridge

"Dear Sears and Roebuck. Please fix our radio and send it right back. We have to travel sixty miles by dog team to get it mailed, and sixty more miles to get it unmailed, and we don't know if there is a war going on or not."

We had listened to daily programs more for the sake of hearing voices than for the programs themselves.

One afternoon when the teakettle was singing on the kitchen stove, Loupe sighing under the table and the radio blah-blahing about Little Nell, Curly went through an elaborate ritual known as "sled fixin'." He brought the sled into the living room, produced a bottle of shellac and a paintbrush, and doctored it a bit. He brought in the hammer, nails, screws, rawhide laces and small pieces of wood. He taped a side piece that had cracked when he did a Steve Brodie on a curve and the sled a loop-the-loop.

"Can you lace this seat for me?" he asked.

"Nope."

"You're going to let me do it all alone?"

"Yup."

He puzzled a while. "Well, how do you think a rawhide star would look in this opening?"

I laid down my knitting. "OK, but don't you ever again say I put soap in the lemon pie."

The round circle of bent ash between the upright handlebars puzzled me when I first saw it, and I was told it was used only on racing sleds. A dog-team driver must end a race with the same number of dogs he started with, and when a dog is too tired to run he is carried in the sled. Going uphill or over hard stretches, the dog is pulled out through the opening and made to walk. He is pushed back in the same way, with the driver having to get off the sled and waste time.

Curly took his rawhide from an old bear paw snowshoe he had picked up in his travels. It was more junk but he unstrung it and the water pails were filled with coils of rawhide to soak and soften. He didn't have enough rawhide, and one of the rawhide laced chairs in the living room disappeared.

Another ritual was cutting the dogs' toenails. The dogs were brought into the camp, and each had his turn at sitting on the bench and having his toenails trimmed. A dog's paws are the most important part of a sled dog, and the most easily injured. If the nails grow too long they will split and be painful and bloody. The pads are sensitive and are easily cut on gravel or crust. We often inspected their paws, and soaked them in salt water.

Loupe had small feet but his paws were well padded and he was never bothered with snowballs gathering between his toes and splitting them. The Siberian husky is a small dog compared to a German shepherd, but he carries better on snow. The pups had large, well-furred paws. They hocked themselves when they were first in harness, but we treated every cut with a coating of fine pitch. They had had one serious fight in their career which had left them both pretty well slashed and quite docile.

That winter, the weather was especially stormy and cold. The mailman snowshoed in from Lac Frontiere only once or twice a month. He had two dogs and a sled to haul the mail-bags, and he stayed with us overnight. What always amazes me about woodsmen is the endurance and vitality they sometimes show at the age of sixty or seventy. The mailman was over sixty years old, and he snowshoed sixty miles in four days to carry the mail. I never could believe that Cyril Jandreau was over fifty. And Mr. Tarr who lived at Clayton was seventy-five, yet he split his winter's wood, shot his deer every fall, and was the best dancer in the country.

The first trip the mailman made was during a freezing, blinding snowstorm. His dogs hadn't been working, and the trip was too hard for them. The smart mongrel leader was only tired, but the other dog, a large black and white husky, had his pads almost torn from his paws, and he left a bloody trail from the burnt land into our camp.

"Key is a good dog, but he is almost finished," the mailman commented that evening.

"Why don't you let us keep him a while, Mr. Caron?" Curly offered. "I'd like to see just how fast those pads can be healed."

"I'll be glad if you do that, but I don't think they will get well quick."

Key was a fine sled dog, strong, willing and friendly, and we liked him. He thought it was great fun to soak his feet in salt water. We kept packs on him, tied him close to a post in the shed where he couldn't walk too much, and gradually trimmed his long toenails. Within two weeks, Key was back in the harness again, and Curly used him with the team.

Real illness was something we never had to cope with, though it was one of the things our friends anticipated with dire prediction. Of course, one of the reasons we had a dog team was for any such emergency that might arise. We just never got sick. We never had colds during the winter—only in the spring when the country opened and strangers brought sniffle noses in with them.

First aid—or what could pass for first aid—had been confined to canine ailments. Once after an eighty-mile trip with the dogs, we noticed a hard lump under Loupe's chin. We didn't think much about it until the next morning when Curly brought him into the camp.

Loupe's head was swollen as large as a water pail. It seemed to be an abscess, probably caused by an old porcupine quill. He couldn't open his jaws, and the swelling reached to his eyes, almost closing them. We had no way of getting him to a veterinary in a hurry, and we hated to think of losing the dog.

"We can try salt pork rind," I suggested.

Curly ransacked the medicine cabinet. "I'd like to lance that, but I don't dare. We'll put hot packs on it, and then wrap it with salt pork."

Loupe sat on the wide bench in the kitchen, flinching every time a freshly heated pack was applied to his chin. He growled when I came too close, but he watched Curly mournfully, as though he knew Curly was trying to help him. I cut a rind from a five-pound piece of salt pork and we bandaged his head with strips from an old sheet. He looked like a dog with a toothache.

"There!" Curly tied a bow knot on the top of his head. "If you could see yourself, you old jughead, you wouldn't feel so bad. If that isn't better this afternoon, I'm going to put you in the sled and have Poo-Poo and the pups haul you to St. Pamphile to see the vet."

Loupe lay on the bench for six hours, hardly changing his position but watching us moving around the kitchen. He lifted his head and whined when we went out of the room. That afternoon, he walked to the sink for a drink of water, and the abscess broke. We left the pork rind on when we went to bed that night, and the next morning he woke Curly by poking his cold nose under the pillow.

But the wound healed too quickly and his chin swelled again. This time Curly cut an incision with a sterilized razor blade and we applied more pork. We kept him in the house for three days, and then let him lead the team, running loose ahead of Pretzel and Beer. He never went too fast, but stopped at curves or forks in the trail and waited for his orders. If he was too far ahead, he ran back and barked at the pups to make them step lively. When his chin healed, he was in the harness again.

The pups had to be wormed every three months, and Loupe and Poo-Poo too, for good measure. Since worm capsules are luxuries of civilization, Curly used the bark from poplar trees—quaking aspen—in their food. He scraped it from poplar twigs, dried it on the back of the stove and crumbled it in their food. Incidentally, it makes good incense too.

Chapter 30

Backwoods Excitement

There is always excitement in the woods. Because we are isolated, a little incident seems tremendous. The all too few
mail days were great occasions. Curly's arrival at the camp after a
week's absence called for the best pot roast, and an airplane that
landed on Churchill Lake was something to talk about for several
days. Some events were really remarkable, such as the morning
Curly was talking to someone over the telephone. During the
conversation he heard a faint voice say "I'm lost! I'm lost!"

He pulled the river switch so he could hear the voice better
and he started to question the person. I could only hear his side
of the conversation and was so excited I burned the toast. I
could hardly wait to hear the whole story.

Pete Pellerin, a World War I veteran and trapper who was
staying at Long Lake dam that winter, was suddenly ill and had
called a plane from Caribou to take him to a hospital. He spent
two weeks in the hospital and was ready to come home—home
being Long Lake dam on the Allagash. The pilot who flew him
back was not familiar with the country, and when a light
snowstorm started he landed on what both he and Pete thought
was Long Lake on the Allagash.

Pete stepped out of the plane and the pilot left immediately, not wishing to be caught in a three- or four-day storm. Pete looked around for his camp and discovered he was on a strange lake. He didn't panic, but he walked all night, all around the lake, exhausted, lost and hungry, and trying to keep from freezing to death.

Toward morning he came across an abandoned fire-warden's camp on the shore of the lake. The windows were gone and porcupines had eaten most of the floor, but the camp had a telephone. The crank was broken and he couldn't ring it, but with the receiver down he might catch someone on the line.

The first person he heard was Curly, and from the description of the lake—a long, narrow lake with an old logging dam at the outlet, and no camps, like many of the lakes between the St. John River and Portage—Curly couldn't tell what lake it might be. He called Dickey Central—Mrs. Charles Henderson who handles all the calls from the forestry lines in that country—and through the network of lines she located Pete on one of the Musquacook lakes. She called a lumber camp at Round Pond to have two men go to Musquacook with a sled and food and bring Pete out.

This was too much excitement for one day and, woman fashion, I was at the telephone telling everyone the news. I talked until late at night.

"For heaven's sake!" Curly interrupted. "Aren't you ever going to stop talking?"

"Hello, Anna, you still there? Curly is making so much noise I can't hear a thing. Yes, add a few bread crumbs and grated cheese."

"I want my supper!" Curly howled.

"Hello, hello—no, it's just that man again. You'll have to bake it quite a while. OK? Bye, I've got to get some supper."

"What in the world were you talking about?" he fumed. "I thought you'd started about Pete Pellerin."

"We did."

"Well, where do the bread crumbs come in? Here I sit starving to death and you spend your time talking about bread crumbs!"

"That was a recipe for leftover potatoes."

"Leftover potatoes! Pete Pellerin! Holy Old Mackinaw! I want some baked potatoes, some asparagus, some meat with lots of gravy and I want some pumpkin pie!"

During March the days were warm and sunny and I spent more time outdoors. The garage intrigued me. I always used to wonder what could keep Curly there when dinner was ready. I tinkered around, gave the emery wheel a spin, looked into the tin cans and boxes, sawed a piece of board he was saving for a canoe bracket, and broke a tooth on the ripsaw.

There was a bare spot in the living room where our rustic rawhide chair had once been, and I decided to build a chair, something to lounge in with my feet on the stove. Curly hooted when I mentioned it, but he hid the ripsaw. I snitched the ax.

I cut two slender birch trees, planning to have a swinging canvas back and seat, built something like a sawhorse with cross-pieces. Green birch is heavy, as I discovered when the two I had cut were lying in the snow with ends looking as though a beaver had chewed them. I couldn't lift them. I went back to camp, harnessed the pups and hauled the logs into the dooryard. I pulled nails and spikes from the old lumber camp above us, measured, sawed, pounded and calmly listened to well-worn advice.

"Pooie, you'd better put the nails in with the pointed ends down or they'll fall out. Maybe you'd better paint the ends of this timber so it won't sprout a tree on us. That would be an awful thing. The birds would be coming into the camp to see the tree, and you know they make an awful mess on the floor."

"You aren't even funny. I've seen you tear your hair when you were building a top shelf."

The graceful curves in the birches were to be matching side pieces, but when it was almost done and the sides were ready to put together with crosspieces—one side slanted one way and the other another—they were so heavy two men couldn't lift them. Anyway, we had enough birch wood to burn in the cookstove for two weeks, and I could subdue Curly by referring to the "cat trapeze." This was a washtub and wringer stand he had built for me to move in and out of the kitchen on Mondays. It sat on the porch because it wouldn't go through the door. Neither would it have collapsed had the bridge fallen on it.

We later bought a "nails not included" chair from a mail-order catalogue for $1.39. Luckily we put it together in the living room—that wouldn't have gone through the door either. The top of the door came just to Curly's nose, and the first time he came into the kitchen with an armload of wood, it knocked him cold. Even I couldn't go through the door without ducking my head, and for a long time after we left Nine Mile, neither of us could go through a doorway without dipping and looking sort of silly.

Chapter 31

Dog Sense

Curly patrolled the boundary from St. Pamphile and Big Black River to Daaquam and the North West Branch on the opposite end. He traveled into Churchill, Clayton, Eagle and Priestly lakes, and sometimes he would be gone five and six days. He didn't have to sleep in the snow—not with a dog team that could average forty miles a day—but both he and the dogs would be considerably thinner when they drove back into the dooryard. It would be so cold outside that the dogs would have to be unharnessed inside the camp, and buckles would be so frosted they were painful to touch with bare hands. Curly pounded his feet and hands while they burned and thawed. "A funny thing happened today," he said. "I fell off the sled, and the moment I hit the ground Loupe swung the team around and was back to where I was."

"What do you suppose he did that for?" I asked.

"That white devil is intelligent. Just to see what he would do, I fell off this afternoon and lay in the snow without moving. He stopped the team and stood right by me, pushing me with his nose and whining. The pups were restless, and say, he was the ugliest dog I ever saw when he turned on them and made them lie down. I stayed there fifteen minutes and he kept nudging me all the time and howling. He nearly went crazy when I stood up and patted him."

"You ought to try it sometime, only lying there longer to see what he will do."

"I've thought of that. I think he'd come home. But I'm not going to try it again. He might think I'm always fooling."

I didn't worry about Curly when he was away. I knew he could take care of himself. He hadn't been a game warden for thirteen years without learning something. But there was always the possibility of his breaking a leg or falling through the ice. When Loupe was with him, I knew he was all right.

One early March morning the trapper across the river awoke us.

"Curly, you've got to take my wife to Lac Frontiere!"

Curly bounced out of bed. "What's the trouble, Brooks?"

"She's going to have a baby!" Brooks was frantic.

"But it isn't time," I said.

"I know," he shrugged, "but she's awful sick."

Curly dressed and drank his coffee while I harnessed the dogs. He threw the sleeping bag in the sled, and within ten minutes he was on his way to get her.

They just flew on their way back. The four dogs were running fast and low. Hermanse huddled in the sleeping bag, and Curly shouted to the dogs. It was fortunate that there was a crust, but he must have driven them furiously because he covered the fifteen miles in two hours—fast time for a heavy load. Of course he couldn't run behind the team at that pace, but he did run up the hills, and he was only two hours ahead of the stork.

I think I hold the record for fast dog trips from Nine Mile to Lac Frontiere. Curly awoke me one morning, not by the usual spider rattling, but by telling me the crust was fine, the weather clear, and I could have the dogs to go to Lac Frontiere for overnight. Within half an hour I was dressed in mukluks, ski pants, parka and leather mittens, and was off over the knoll on the road to Lac Frontiere.

It was more than a fine day. It was beautiful and snappy cold. Bright sunlight sparkled on the icy crust. I sang, shouted and whooped to my heart's delight. Loupe turned around four times and each time we had a tussle in the snow before he went on.

Going down the last hill into Lac Frontiere I met an ox team on its way to a maple-sugar camp. The dogs spotted it and we flew down the hill. I pressed on the brakes—a long strip of ash that was tipped with a pronged piece of steel—and shouted *whoa*!

The dogs slowed only because I was stepping so hard on the brake. The ox team had pulled to the side of the road to let us by, but Loupe had different ideas. He stopped directly in front of the team and crouched in the snow. For a long second I was paralyzed. I remembered his killer record and expected him to leap, bringing in the whole team and the devil to pay.

I dragged the whip from the knapsack, uncoiled it over their backs with a *swoosh,* and shouted "ALL RIGHT!"

Loupe jumped sideways and sailed past. I often wondered afterward if I looked as stunned as the man in the ox sled. His jaw was hanging open and his eyes popped.

I left the dogs at the mailman's place, went overtown, shopped and called on Hermanse. She was still laughing about Curly's experience with the midwives.

It seems that Hermanse's father insisted that all the dogs be brought into the house and fed raw hamburger. He wanted to thank them for saving his daughter's life. A birth in a French Canadian range-road home is not necessarily a private affair, and the four dogs, two midwives and the neighbors had the run of the place. Every time Hermanse yelled, the four dogs came into the room to see what was going on. The midwives left hurriedly through the nearest door, at this intrusion of danger, and Poo-Poo lapped Hermanse's face in sympathy. Curly would come in to drive the dogs out, while the neighbors drove the midwives back in through another door. The only ones who didn't think it was funny were Curly and the two midwives.

The next morning I was on the road at six o'clock. The weather was as fine as the day before, and the crust had frozen harder, holding sled and dogs. We whooped over the hills, skidding on the curves. Loupe was running fast and low to get home to Curly as quickly as possible, and just an hour and twenty minutes later the team pulled into the dooryard. They were breathless, and my legs and wrists ached from balancing. I say I hold the record, but it was really Loupe. It was the fastest ride I ever had with the team, and the most exciting.

Chapter 32

The Ice Goes Out

We were sitting on the porch absorbing the late April sunshine. It was quiet and we heard the soft, almost imperceptible settling of the snow, almost sighing as it melted in the hot sun. Water dripped from the eaves of the camp. The dogs wandered back and forth along their wires, rattling their chains and occasionally glancing toward us. For several days the weather had been clear and sunny, and the snow was melting fast.

We wondered when the ice would go out of the river. Narciss wanted to know how his new bulkhead on the bridge would stand the pounding, and Seven Islands wanted to know so they could move to the mainland before being flooded.

I had never seen the ice go out at Nine Mile and neither had Curly. We had heard descriptions of it. We knew what to expect and were ready to move out of the camp should the water rise too high. The year before, the three trappers had been at Nine Mile. When they heard the roar of the ice going out, one of them, who was in the midst of a shaving operation, ran out of the camp, with lather still on his face. He raced the half mile to the bridge and tore across it just as the ice hit. He dropped his razor and picked up speed, not wishing to be caught on the wrong side of the river in case the bridge went out.

On the first of April we chose the date the ice would run. My date, optimistically, was April twenty-seventh, and Curly's was May first. Written on a board above the door at Nine Mile were the dates the ice has run for the past eight years. It has been known to go out as early as March and as late as the tenth of May. Today was the twenty-seventh of April, and I still thought my chances were good. The river ice was yellowish, colored from the rising muddy water beneath it.

In Fort Kent, we always went to the International Bridge to see the ice run in the St. John River, and the log drive behind it. One year the town was flooded, and canoes and outboard motors were used on Main Street. There was no school and the kids built rafts and paddled all over the place. Someone kept a cow in the cellar and it was drowned.

We didn't expect a great flood of water on the upper part of the St. John River. We thought the ice would run smoothly, as it did a hundred miles down the river.

"Listen!" I stood up.

"Sounds like a motor, but it must be a big one."

"It's the river!" I shouted.

Curly started for the bridge. "The ice is going out!"

I raced after him. The ice was going out!

There wasn't much to see at first, but soon the faint roar became thunderous and angry. A ten-foot wall of tumbling, crackling, fast-moving ice rolled around the upper bend of the river, sweeping everything before it, gathering momentum and throwing two-ton ice floes on the high banks. It uprooted trees and crumbled the fettered ice sheet in its path. The dammed water behind pushed relentlessly, increasing in force and power, and coming closer and closer.

It was greenish white, and some of the packed, moving ice cakes reflected the sun's rays in rainbow colors. As far as we could see, this massed ice plateau was surging—rising as high as the riverbanks.

It was breathtaking, and I hung tightly to the bridge railing, unable to tear my eyes away. The ten-foot wall grew to twelve feet, then to fifteen, and thirty feet from the bridge it angrily greeted us with an ear-splitting screech. Curly touched my arm and I turned away. The spell was broken and we started to run.

We just stepped off the bridge as the ice struck. The iron girders quivered and the ground around us was shaken. From the knoll I stopped to look back, thinking it had surely carried away the bridge. But with a muffled rumbling it ground its way slowly between the piers. Large cakes smashed and splintered on the new cement facing of the middle pier. Logs were ripped from the sides of the bridgeheads as though they were kindling. Ice cakes were thrown over the railing.

The momentum was slowed for a moment as the quarter-mile-long and hundred-yard-wide mass of ice tore a channel down the river. Twenty feet of ice was piled on our lawn and cut off the view. Logs and uprooted trees that were caught in the maelstrom tossed about like chips. The bridge held—had it gone out, so would the camp. It was then I remembered to call Seven Islands and warn them.

We went back to the bridge to watch. The water level rose fifteen feet. "Just look at that ice sheet!" Curly exclaimed. "It must be seventy feet across!"

"See the deer tracks on it!"

The ice sheet curved upward on the middle pier, shuddered and broke into two channels.

At noon the river was clearer, whispering, swishing and running fast. The masses of ice came down less frequently and were smaller in size. I went back to the camp for a bite to eat, and Curly stayed on the bridge for another look. I heard him shout and then saw him run down to the lawn. "There's a deer out there!"

I climbed over the ice cakes on the bank and saw a dead fawn floating down the river. A short way behind it was a doe, barely able to keep her head above water. We got axes from the shed and slashed a path through the ice bank. Curly dragged the canoe over while I brought out a paddle and rope.

The fawn had caught on a shelf of ice that was still clinging to the opposite shore, but the doe had gone by the camp. Curly started after her. I watched as he quickly overtook the deer and tried to lift her into the canoe. She fought wildly, and they drifted closer to the rapids that would smash them over and over against the rocks.

He tied the rope around her neck, looped it around the back thwart of the canoe, and paddled like mad toward the flat sheet of ice that hadn't been dislodged from the cove above the rapids. He jumped out as soon as the canoe touched, and dragged both canoe and deer on the ice.

I had been running along the bank and I helped him pull the deer out of the water. "You stay here," he said. "I'm going back for the outboard motor. If this ledge starts to go, don't stop for anything. Run for the bank."

When Curly came back he put the motor on the canoe and between the two of us we lifted the deer in. I grabbed the paddle in the bow and he pushed off. The moment he did, the sheet of ice broke away. It was caught in the current—nearly taking

us with it—and was pounded to pieces in the rapids that were
so close. The motor started with the first crank—thanks to his
persistent, careful and frequent overhauling—and we were clear.
"OK, Pooie," he shouted above the roaring of the motor. "You
can drop the paddle now, but keep an eye on the deer."

"We're all right now," I shouted.

"We are if no more ice cakes come down."

We were back at our landing in no time, and had to chop
more ice before we could drag the canoe and the deer onto
the lawn.

The doe was motionless, paralyzed with cold, but still alive.
Her eyes were glassy as though she had lost consciousness. She
had been badly bruised from encounters with the sharp ice, and
was bleeding through several open wounds. We laid a woods
spread on the ground, dragged the deer onto it, and covered her
with a blanket. Curly called my attention to her eyes. "She's
watching us. See her roll her eyes when we move."

"Maybe if we fed her something warm she would feel better."

"Try warm milk with salt in it."

I pried her jaws open and poured the milk down her throat.
Within a few hours she was on her feet, eating cookies, drinking
milk from a pan, and fighting the dog collar and chain we had
put on her. Curly rushed her with a woods spread to protect
himself from her flying hoofs. He knocked her down and
unloosed the collar. The dogs were in an uproar, but the deer
soon realized that they couldn't touch her, and she paid no
attention to them.

When she was free, she still stayed around us, taking a few
wobbly steps, shaking her head and drinking milk from the pan
I held in my hands. For twenty minutes she lingered in the

dooryard, hardly moving; then she walked over the knoll and into the woods, glancing back every few steps.

She was a frequent visitor that summer. We often saw her standing on the knoll, watching the camp. She was there when we left the country and was easily recognized because of the deep scar on her right ribs.

In all the excitement I had forgotten that I'd won my bet. "I won!" I yelled. "I won!"

Curly jumped. "Won what?"

"You know, my pinking scissors. Those scissors to cut little triangles on the edge of cloth. This is the twenty-seventh, and this is the day I said the ice would run!"

Chapter 33

Whitewater

The road opened May first. Most of the snow that year was between Nine Mile and Clayton. There was three feet of it there when there wasn't any from Clayton to Churchill. Joe Deblois surprised everyone, including himself, when he drove from Churchill to Clayton in his little Ford sedan.

I was sitting on our porch one early spring morning when I noticed a whiff of smoke coming from the bridge. I ran to the bridge to investigate and discovered that a fire had started in the planking. I ran back to camp and frantically rang the telephone, trying to call the fire warden who has a camp near Nine Mile. There was no answer, and I jumped into the car and drove to his camp, thinking he might be working outside. The camp was empty.

I was alone at Nine Mile. Curly had gone down the river with his canoe, and I was frightened. The weather had been so dry that the woods were like dry tinder. I called the Druins on the phone and started hauling pails of water to the bridge. By that time the flames were leaping four feet high, and every time I carried two more pails of water on the bridge, I found that flames had erupted someplace else. I did make headway though, and when Narciss and two men arrived, the fire was under control.

I had never been so close to being caught in a forest fire. I had seen many of them when I was a youngster, and when forest fires were common events and considered inevitable. The Forestry Service wasn't the organization that it is today. I was nine years old when I saw my first forest fire, and to this day I can't look at a picture of one without shuddering and remembering that awful roaring.

The fire wardens weren't far behind Narciss, and since only one car had been in over the road that morning, they had no trouble finding the culprit who threw the lighted cigarette out of the car window. The sportsmen, or "nonresidents" as Curly calls them, were asked to leave the country. We feel very possessive about our woods. The miscreants were more frightened of the black looks on everyone's faces than they were of the damage that had been caused by the cigarette.

Curly sighted the smoke downriver and was back at camp within a few hours, but I couldn't play the role of the heroine for very long. He had something else on his mind. "Pack a grub box, Pooie! We're going to Ross Lake!"

"You mean we're really going?"

"Yup. The water is just right."

I hustled about the kitchen, collecting tin plates and canned foods. "At last I'm going to see that place!"

Curly had often been there, and I had heard much about Ross Lake, as it is called. Its real name is Chemquassabamticook Lake, a genuine tongue twister. If you take it in syllables, it is easy—Chem-quas-sa-bam-ti-cook.

Chemquassabamticook Stream—or Sebemsicook Stream—is usually impassable because it dwindles to the shallowest trickle in the summertime. On a spring freshet, the "trickle" is a full-grown, respectable river.

We planned to stay overnight and try the fishing; we loaded the canoe on the car and threw in the sleeping bag, blankets, outboard motor, gasoline and fishing tackle. We drove to Clayton Lake and unloaded again at the landing. When we were on our way at last, with the motor purring, and short, choppy waves slapping the bow of the canoe, it was just ten o'clock in the morning.

At the mouth of Sebemsicook Stream, the lake is marshy and more like bog water. The stream is a wide avenue through the reeds, and we had no sooner swung into it when we felt the powerful force of the current. I was surprised because bog water is usually smooth and easygoing. This looked smooth, but the water was running much faster than I thought it could run. The momentum it had gathered in its drop down the mountainside carried it along, and reeds in its path were flattened.

Proceeding up the river we left the bog behind, and the water gathered into a distinct riverbed. Alders grew along the shore, but they gradually gave way to dark-green spruce as the banks became steeper. The forest was dark and thick, with thin beams of daylight showing through. Ancient cedars had long, dangling beards of moss.

The swiftness of the current had slowed us considerably, and we seemed to crawl around the sharp, winding bends as we went deeper and deeper under the giant trees. The wind blew in gusts, snaking between an opening in the trees and pushing us back. I grabbed a paddle in the bow and helped swing the canoe around to head into the channel again. Curly ran the motor wide open and shouted, "Come on, bend the maple! We want to get there before we need a lantern!"

By noon we had gone only four miles, the easiest four in the whole fourteen-mile trip. We stopped at a trapper's cabin and ate our lunch, slapped black flies, boiled water for tea and smoked before starting again. A new sponson canoe was beached on the shore. "Must be strangers," I remarked, needlessly.

"Guess they walked in," Curly said. "They couldn't have taken much with them. This canoe is well loaded."

"They must have known they couldn't get anywhere with a canoe like that."

"My dear Mrs. Know-it-all," Curly said. "How would the average sportsman know that this is one of the roughest rivers in the state? Very few people know that it even exists."

The river narrowed from there on. At its widest it was fifteen feet, and at its narrowest four feet. Occasionally we cut away the fallen trees that were lying across the stream, but we could duck under those that were held three or four feet above the water by the thick growth on the opposite bank. Before we reached the seven miles of rapids, the roar of them surrounded us. The landscape was no longer dark and mysterious. Scraggly trees were clinging to reddish, barren rock. Sheer cliffs and enormous boulders had been thrown there by some giant hand. The sunlight was bright.

The silent stream was now a raging torrent beating against caging rock walls, swirling angrily around the boulders and tumbling hastily down the uneven riverbed. In the sunlight the water was white, sparkling and foamy, changing yet ever the same. The same ripple was left over a jutting rock when the water had moved on. The same water spread over shallow bars and gathered between narrow banks.

We pulled close to shore to let the motor cool, while Curly studied the sweep of the current to pick out his channel. I stared, amazed at the combative desires it aroused in me. I had seen whitewater before—wild and tempestuous—but I wanted to tear through this storm, to shout as loudly as the falling water.

"What do you think of it?" Curly asked.

"I'm surprised. It really goes downhill, doesn't it?"

"You'll think so when we get into it."

He started the motor, and at full speed we inched our way forward, crept up behind rocks, shot around them with a quick jerk and the canoe settled and slowed in the faster water. We rounded the turns on the inside bank, and with another quick jerk we were stationary as the motor held its own against the current. Before we had gone a mile we were drenched with spray and were clinging to the scrubby bushes on the quieter shore to let the motor cool again. I bailed out the four inches of water in the bottom of the canoe.

Our progress was slow but steady. The canoe rocked easily, swinging back and forth in the rough water. On shallow shoals there wasn't enough water for the motor shaft, and Curly tipped it forward—raising the propeller a bit. When it did strike bottom the canoe quivered with the shock. Sometimes we moved slowly along the edge of a sheer rock cliff, and sometimes we would be stopped for ten minutes on a rolling pitch. Curly grabbed the setting pole, and with one hand he pushed us ahead.

The last mile was quiet as the water spread over a wide, sandy riverbed, and at five o'clock in the afternoon we sighted the old wooden dam on Ross Lake.

The dam held most of the water in the lake, but it had broken through at one end and a waterfall swept in a curve between it and the bank. We hauled the canoe onto the open bank and over the dam into the lake. I couldn't have been more tired if I'd done all the work, but Curly was jubilant. He had "made good time"—fourteen miles in seven hours.

There is an old trapper's cabin on Ross Lake, and we packed our equipment over the trail. The trapper who built the cabin was a well-known French Canadian, Gus Bernier, who earned his living by poaching beavers and eluding game wardens. He could walk miles with practically nothing to eat, and he defied anyone to catch him. Once he was across the border, he was safe.

He was caught just once, and two game wardens made him walk to Fort Kent. They watched Gus day and night, to see that he didn't slip into the woods and disappear. He was a poor man, couldn't pay his fine, and had to stay in jail.

He still lives in Lac Frontiere, and I once met him. He was an old man, stocky and stoop shouldered from carrying heavy packs all his life. His face was lined and weather-beaten, and his hands curled with rheumatism. Untidy, matted hair escaped from a rakish wool cap, and his eyes were watery and squinting. He hardly looked the part—a poacher pirate—but he was a headache to the game wardens. His feet are now so crippled from continuous frostbite that his activities are limited close to home. Ironically, his "outlaw" hideout on Ross Lake is used as a stopping place by the game wardens.

On the short trail to camp, we met one of the fishermen. "Holy Moses," he excitedly greeted us, "how did you get here?"

"Canoe."

"If you came through there with a canoe, I want to see it!"

"You don't think we lugged these heavy packs fourteen miles!"

He was one of the party of four fishermen who had abandoned the heavy sponson we had seen on the river, and had walked to Ross Lake over the partially up-grown tote road. He led the way back to the camp we had planned to occupy, and before opening the door, he called, "Hey, Joe, put on your pants, there's a lady here."

"Aw, go on, that ain't no lady, that's my wife."

"OK, don't say I didn't warn you."

Someone looked out of a window and a hurried scramble took place inside before the heavy door swung open to admit us. The camp was large and low ceilinged, and in the dim light all I could see were the pole bunks, an oil-barrel stove and a dirt floor. The camp had been built quite a time ago—the logs were some of the virgin timber still left in the country. It was chinked with rags, mud and moss, and there were but two small windows that were covered with oiled paper.

The sportsmen had had such a hard trek over the tote road that they hadn't been able to carry much food. Their larder was low, and we pooled our resources. Since they occupied the camp, they set up a pup tent for us and built a bough bed. I went to bed early that night, and left the men to talk their hunting and fishing as they inevitably and always do.

Curly is as bad as any of them. He doesn't care particularly about hunting, but he would rather fish than eat, and will gladly talk about it for hours while I impatiently wait and listen to the usual fish story that some wild-eyed fisherman has to tell.

"My God, that was a beautiful salmon that I hooked at Moosehead, wasn't it, Joe? Say, that thing come out of the water and he took that silver doctor—just like that" (snapping of fingers), "didn't he, Joe? It weighed fourteen pounds if it weighed an ounce. Ask Joe, he can tell you. He was right there. Say, when that salmon jumped, I'll swear he was three feet long. Wasn't he, Joe? My God, that was a beautiful salmon. Three feet long! Say, I played him for twenty minutes. My rod was bent just like that" (tracing of arc in ozone), "wasn't it, Joe? I had him right up to the boat and was going to net him when the barstard got away! My God, that was a beautiful salmon!"

The next morning we fished, and I had a chance to inspect the lake. Few companies have cut there, and during the long intervals between, the spruces have grown tall again, hiding the traces of man's destruction. The dam is gradually rotting away, and the dri-ki has completely disappeared from the flooded shores. The lake is a thousand feet above sea level. It is almost five miles long and is two miles wide, and has one sandy beach. Except for the ruins of an earlier lumber camp, the lake is wild and lonely. There are no hills to be seen in the distance, only the dark ring of spruce.

The Ross Lake togue are not as pretty as the togue we catch in Eagle Lake. They are darker, longer and thinner. Such togue are often miscalled "racers," which really are skinny fish. An inspection of their stomach contents reveals colored rocks, twigs and bark. Because Ross Lake has no real inlets, it has little fish food—smelts, for instance. Probably if these racers were well fed, they would be lighter in color and heavier.

We kept one togue and on our way back to camp caught a beautiful mess of trout below the dam. The morning had been windy and the lake was choppy; we spent most of our time along the shores, just poking and looking.

I hated to leave that afternoon, and I could easily understand why Gus Bernier preferred being a renegade. The lake is a gem on a mountaintop. During the winter it must be lonely and desolate when the wind howls across the white sheet of frozen ice, sweeping snowy swirls and drifts before it, and forcing the tall spruces to bow before its superior strength. But what could be cozier in comparison than a warm cabin, a fire flickering in the stove and reddish light escaping from around loosely fitted stove plates and from the open grate to dance on the gigantic logs.

In the fall it must be lovely when the dark ring of spruce is flecked with color, as the insignificant maples and beeches commence to assert themselves. The only visitors would be shelldrakes, or *she-cor-ways,* as the Indians named them.

If the trip upriver had been slow, the ride down most certainly was anything but. We flew—leaping ahead of the current, ducking between rolling swells, dodging around the huge rocks and tossing in the seething water. My hands gripped the gunwales, and my knees were bent and braced to jump if we should crash on those cliffs. Curly whistled cheerily in the stern as we raced around one bend after another, down mile after mile until we were in the "deadwater" again and speeding toward Clayton Lake.

In an hour and a half we were back at the landing. I was still unsettled after the experience, not frightened, but my knees were surprisingly wobbly. I jabbered excitedly, "Let's go back and come down again!"

"Sorry, Pooie, that's the last of the spring freshet."

"But can't we get up after a rain?"

"I wish it could be done, but the next trip I make there, I'll have to pole and wade. Can't motor up there again this year."

For days afterward I could visualize that frenzied, riotous river boiling down the mountainside, imprisoned by the restraining gorges, and offering up lofty spumes of rainbow spray to the Gods of Anger in its one short week of yearly indulgence.

Chapter 34

River Trips

I never went back to Chemquassabamticook Lake, and I probably wouldn't care to now. A sportsman's camp was built
there recently, and airplanes come and go in defiance of nature's
barriers. I much prefer to think of the "outlaw" camp, a monu-
ment to stubbornness and backbreaking work.

Many fishermen came into the country by plane. They can
easily reach ponds and lakes that it would take days to walk to,
or paddle. The Musquacook, Cliff, Clear, Pleasant, Ross and
Harrow lakes are good for a limit of trout because they aren't
fished often. Albino trout were caught in Clear Lake.

Some fishermen came into the country by car, if they could
get a permit to go over the private road. Puzzled fishermen
called at the camp and inquired if the game warden lived there.

"Yes," I answered, "but he isn't home now. Is there anything
I can do for you?"

"We are looking for a camp we can rent."

"I'm sorry, but there are no camps for rent. There is a boardinghouse at Churchill where you might be able to stay."

"But we want to hire guides and canoes," they insisted.

"The only guides I know, two of them, are booked a year ahead. I'm afraid you're out of luck. There aren't any canoes for rent either."

Many a fishing trip was ruined because the fishermen hadn't taken the trouble to find out about the place they were going to.

Canoe enthusiasts made the Allagash and St. John River trips, and we met many boys' camps with their ten and twelve canoes, veteran guides and scantily clothed, suntanned and laughing boys on a real Maine woods vacation. The chief advantage of the Allagash trip is the long distance that can be traveled on water, starting at Moosehead Lake and traveling by canoe as far as Fort Kent. Many of the lakes have been dammed and flooded to hold a supply of water to use for driving logs, and the shores are lined with dri-ki, making it difficult to beach a canoe. Some thoroughfares between lakes are real fairylands. In the summer the water lilies smell heavenly, and to see them with the blue irises and pink primroses that grow on the marshy banks makes you think that you have intruded into the jewel-encrusted playground of an elfin princess.

The Allagash River—*Allagash* means hemlock bark—is tranquil and quiet compared to the St. John River. The land is flat, and there are channels through rocky and rough places. The river is so controlled by logging dams that it no longer pounds furiously down the waterways, a characteristic that gave it its reputation. Of course not everyone can successfully make the Allagash trip without a competent guide who is familiar with the channel as well as the ways of water.

The first trip I made on the Allagash was during a blinding rainstorm. Curly was called to Fort Kent, and I had to go too. We left in the morning, shrouded in raincoats, gum rubbers and old felt hats that we had found in the barn at Umsaskis. We didn't stop anywhere, but ate our lunch when we carried over the falls. "I don't know why I need this raincoat," I remarked, pulling off my boots and emptying the water out.

"It is drizzling a bit today, isn't it? These peanut butter sandwiches are soggy."

"Soggy! I think they are waterlogged. I packed some cookies but I can't find them. They must have floated off."

A warden at Allagash drove us into Fort Kent by car, and we walked up Main Street with boots squeaking and slushing at every step. Our blue jeans were wet and clammy, and water dripped from the brims of the old hats. We were disreputable, shaggy and in high spirits, and I couldn't imagine why no one recognized me. I did hear the comment—"Moosetowners!"

That amuses me. The residents of Fort Kent call the residents of Allagash "Moosetowners," although eighty percent of the population of Fort Kent were once lumberjacks. It isn't eighty percent now, only fifty—the rest raise potatoes.

We went up the Allagash River at night, guided by the white shirt of Warden Hallie Dow who led the way in his canoe. The Allagash River is Hallie's back dooryard, and he could run it blindfolded. It's a funny sensation not to see the rough places until you're in them and feel the canoe rocking in the swells.

We carried over the falls at midnight. I stepped along gingerly with a loaded packsack on my shoulders, a gasoline can in one hand and two paddles in the other, trying to feel out the path in the inky blackness. We slept at Hallie's camp below Round Pond, and continued on our way the next morning. On later excursions I was able to appreciate the beauties of the Allagash River on a clear, sunny day.

The St. John River trip is wilder and more arduous and should never be attempted if the water is low. Canoes have to be dragged over sandbars and rock ledges and get badly cut. Only an experienced canoeman can make the trip, even if the water is high. The St. John is long. The upper hundred miles of river are entirely in the state of Maine. From St. Francis to Grand Falls, the St. John is the international boundary, and from there until it flows into the Bay of Fundy it is entirely in New Brunswick. The Reversible Falls at the mouth of the St. John are a last outburst of rebellion before the river flows into the Atlantic.

Each quarter mile of the upper St. John River produces whitewater, and few men have run Big Black Rapids at its highest pitch. The river is wild and rocky, practically untouched by the hand of man, and still in its natural, boisterous state. It is unhampered by logging dams, and the water level rises and falls with every slight rainfall or spell of dry weather.

Whitewater is bewitching. One of the biggest thrills in life, to me, is to be able to watch an expert canoeman handle a setting pole. I don't wish to insinuate that Curly is an expert with a setting pole. Compared to Dave Jackson he is an amateur.

Many people are familiar with a paddle, but few know what a setting pole is. A rookie game warden once described it in an examination as the place where the game warden sits to watch for poachers. But I shouldn't laugh. I didn't know what it was either, until I lived on the Allagash. I once remarked to Curly that the "pickpole" that was in the shed was blocking traffic.

"What did you call it?" he asked.

"A pickpole."

"You'd better not let anyone else hear you call it that. It's a setting pole."

"But aren't they the same thing?"

"I guess not! A pickpole is what lumberjacks use on the drive. I can see that your education has been neglected."

A setting pole is a slender, lancelike, pliant pole about fifteen feet long. It is a small tree whittled and peeled to from one to one and a half inches in diameter, thicker in the middle where pressure is exerted, and tipped with a blunted pick. A pickpole is not as delicately balanced, and has a sharp pick on the end to spear logs.

The canoeman stands in the stern of his twenty-foot canoe, sliding the setting pole through his hands, settling the blunted pick firmly on the river bottom, and pushing gently and smoothly and slowly, sometimes motionless, but advancing without seeming to exert effort.

Dropping downstream is a series of snubs, stopping the canoe in its rush with the current by setting—bracing with the setting pole, from which it gets its name. It sounds simple. I know. I tried it. The canoe swung around and I was leaning on air. The setting pole bounced and so did I—right into the water. And I had to chase the confounded canoe for half a mile down the river.

Although outboard motors are used, there are still occasions when a setting pole is the only and absolutely necessary means of transportation. Traveling on the rivers has changed as much with the outboard motors as the rivers themselves have been changed by logging dams. Outboard motors are fast and easy to handle, and heavier loads are carried with little effort. It isn't as romantic as the old way, but by no means to be belittled. It calls for the same experience with river temperaments as the setting pole does, and for quicker thinking in tight spots.

After a breathless ride through a quarter-mile stretch of whitewater, riding the swells and following an unseen channel, I asked Curly how he knew he could get between those last two boulders.

"Don't you know?"

"No."

"When the water beats between the rocks, it clears a channel deep enough for a canoe."

I have traveled many miles on the rivers, and I have come to the conclusion that a whitewater man learns the "color" of water. Dangerous places look threatening. The water is loud and angry, and pushes in all directions as it tries to force a way through the rocky channel. It is grayish as it does not reflect any certain color. It is white tipped and frothy with temper.

Easy water has a gay and tinkly pattern, reflecting the blue of the skies and a touch of green from the landscape. It is shiny where it reflects all the light. Shallow water is light in color and deep water has deeper shades. If the riverbed is smooth, the surface has brownish tints mixed with the blues and greens.

Little tracers of foam will follow a channel where the water has cleared a path for itself. Water will ripple over a covered rock, bulging and circling in the backwash. Nearly always a channel will follow the inside bank and swing to the opposite shore on a curve.

A whitewater man is probably familiar with only a few of the many rough rivers in the state of Maine, but experience will teach him how to run anything anywhere. In the old days they used bateaus, large flat-bottom scows, and pirogues, long, slender boats hewn from a giant tree, to follow the lumber drives. Canoes were the gift of the Algonquin and Chippewa Indians, and the smallest of the real Indian canoes was twenty-five feet long. I shudder when I see those "sissy" fifteen- and sixteen-foot canoes. A river man will always use a twenty-foot canoe, if not longer.

Lakes are another matter; they have to be taken seriously, as they change aspect with the weather. A lake may be calm, serene and inviting, mirroring the blue skies, and half an hour later be choppy as shifting winds beat cross waves. It is gray and leaden, and pounds into white-capped waves that race with the blowing gale. I know many whitewater men who are leery of lakes, especially a large one. Surprisingly few of them can swim, and most of them do not like to paddle. Where they can't reach bottom with a setting pole, they feel insecure.

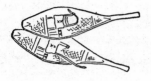

Chapter 35
Old Times

S ome of the few historical facts about this country are interesting. The native Indians of this part of the country were
the Algonquins, and the St. Francis tribe was called the
Abenaki, or Wabanaki, which means People of the Dawn.
Where Big Black River empties into the St. John, the high
clearing overlooking the river is an old Indian camping and bur-
ial ground. Many Indian graves have been excavated there, and
even today bones and relics are found. The people who live on
the river believe that the place is haunted. It has been suggested
that this was once the camping ground for the warlike
Mohawks, to whom the Algonquins paid tribute, and who left
traces of their savagery in these superstitions.

The Indian names of some of the lakes and rivers are strange
sounding, and I wish I knew the meaning of them. I once saw an
old map that had the Indian names of the lakes and rivers on it.
The St. John was called the Wallastook. Big Black River was
Chinkaza-ook. Priestly Lake was Awangonis. Harrow Lake was
Megk-wak-a-gamoosis. Eagle Lake was Pongokwahemook.
Churchill Lake was Allagaskwigamook, which might possibly
mean "home of the Allagash River." Pleasant Lake was

Mahklicongamoc, and Chamberlain Lake was Apmoojenegamook, which means "lake that is crossed"—old landmarks in a forgotten wilderness.

On Long Lake there are the remains of the Harvey Farm. Old Man Harvey cleared a farm in the heart of the woods. He bought his supplies and groceries in Patten, Maine, traveling by pirogue through Churchill, Eagle, Chamberlain, Webster, Second and Grand lakes.

Seven Islands on the St. John River was settled by squatter's rights, as were most of the small settlements and farms in that section. The original settlers of Seven Islands were French Canadians who came down the St. Francis River and up the St. John to build their homes on Seven Islands.

A settlement of French Canadians lived fourteen miles above Big Rapids. They were called the Castonian settlement, and they came originally from East Lake on the boundary. The colony was once considered to be tough, but it has died out now, leaving behind only a few bunkhouse sagas of the wild Castonian lumberjacks.

Not much is known and nothing was ever written about the Allagash settlement. Most of the facts come from an old-timer whose grandfather was one of the first settlers. During the War of 1812, the English colonists who were living at Campbellton on the Baie Chaleur were constantly raided and annoyed by piratical sailing vessels. A group of the colonists left their homes in search of freedom from these persecutions. They traveled on the Restigouche River, following the water highways and portaging where necessary until they entered the St. John and finally settled at the mouth of the Allagash. It is true that some of their descendants have intermingled with the French, but an amazing number of them are still "thoroughbreds." They are different. Their dialect is soft and slurring, and they are reserved and quiet.

In the old days the Allagash people ran a towboat business on the river. They had large, flat scows with cabins on them, and they were towed up the river by horses. The boats were about nine feet wide and fifty feet long, and they carried as much as five tons of supplies to the lumber camps.

Tramway on Eagle Lake is a lumber-camp ghost town, and it is connected with quite an interesting lumber squabble between Canada and the United States, before Civil War times. The thoroughfare between Chamberlain Lake, which originally emptied into Eagle Lake, was a bone of contention between the American lumber barons and the Canadian government.

The Americans built a dam between Chamberlain Lake and Eagle Lake, to get the water to run down the Penobscot River. It was called Lock Dam because it locked the water from Eagle Lake, and therefore lumber could be driven down to Bangor instead of down the international waters of the St. John River where the Crown could collect taxes on it. The dam has been dynamited in its history, and a guard was kept there all the time. Even after the Webster-Ashburton Treaty, the existence of Lock Dam still rankled in the hearts of a few French Canadians.

Hollingsworth and Whitney, a lumber company, built the first settlement at Tramway. They brought in two miles of cable that was cut into short lengths to be handled easily, and they set an engine on the Chamberlain side to run an endless chain across the narrow strip of land. It was an inexpensive way to carry pulpwood from one watershed to the other. It was running in 1903, and the last of the engine can still be found on the shore of Chamberlain Lake.

When La Croix lumbered there he built a railroad from Eagle Lake to the meadows at Chesuncook Lake, the headwaters for the West Branch of the Penobscot River, to drive pulpwood through that part of the state. It always seemed odd to me to think that here in the middle of the woods was a railroad that ran from nowhere to nowhere.

Machinery, boxcars, rails, lumber, engines and men were brought in on the ice and across country from Clayton Lake. No one lives at Tramway now except a few fire wardens during the summer, and La Croix's weather-beaten, white clapboard buildings, rusty equipment and railroad have not been used for a long time.

The Allagash and St. John rivers have been lumbered for a long time, although the country still looks as wild as during frontier times. Huge timbers were cut, hewed square in the woods, and driven down the rivers to be used to build the fort at Fort Kent during the Bloodless Aroostook War.

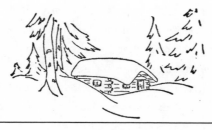

Chapter 36

The Snow Flies Again

The weather had been extremely cold and the ground froze early. The country changed overnight when ten inches of snow fell in the month of October. It was an enchanted world that sparkled on a cold, sunny morning, and we hurried through breakfast and went out to enjoy the newness and strangeness.

"It is really winter again, isn't it?" Curly said.

"Do you mind?" I asked.

"No, not if you don't. I like to see it come but I can't help thinking that downriver October isn't considered a winter month."

I was going to have a baby. I don't know whether I was scared or happy. Mostly happy, I guess. After all, millions of women had babies. Curly, of course, tried to convince me I should spend the winter downriver. I preferred Nine Mile. At least there wouldn't be any neighbors to call and offer "sound advice"—do's and dont's and reminiscences about their own experiences. I could sleep and rest, and knit bootees without the usual comment.

I was going to do everything just as I had always done. The doctor hadn't seemed worried about my being snowbound for six months, and I saw no reason why I should be.

I shot my deer that fall and dressed it myself, but when I made mincemeat, I decided I didn't care for venison. There was only one thing in the world that I wanted to eat, and that was cottage cheese, something I couldn't get or make.

As fast as I knitted bootees, Curly wanted to appropriate them for Loupe. The sleeves in the sweaters I knitted were all too small, and I never used the tiny mittens.

At times I wondered whether *I* was having the baby or Curly. "You're sure you feel all right?" he asked over the breakfast table.

"Of course I feel all right. Why shouldn't I? Don't be a silly. Eat your breakfast."

"Well, if you're sure you feel all right, I feel better too. What's the matter with these eggs?"

"Nothing. They're just the same as we had last winter. Don't you feel all right?"

"I'm not very hungry. Just give me a cup of coffee. Think I'll go outside for a minute."

I ate the six scrambled eggs and bacon.

The first question he invariably asked when getting home from a trip was, "Have you got a bellyache?"

"No, why?"

"Well, I think I've got one."

"You goon! If you mention bellyache again I'll feed you castor oil!"

Curly was busy keeping his trails open with the dogs and shoveling out the ever-increasing snow in the dooryard. When the dogs were home and I needed the cobwebs blown away, I took them for their ten- or twelve-mile exercise run. I once tried Poo-Poo with the skis. The first part of the ride was grand, but when I stopped to turn him around, and he had a good look at the overgrown banana peelings, Poo-Poo decided they were something to get away from. We went back to camp. I wouldn't let go of the rope I had tied to his traces. The skis wouldn't stay uncrossed, and I wouldn't stay upright. My parka filled with snow and Poo-Poo apologized by chewing the fur off my hood when he hit the dooryard.

I often used the pups with the skis. They didn't mind them, but they thought that every time I fell down it meant that I wanted to play. I spent most of the time untangling them, untangling my feet, and tangling up and down the road.

No one skis in this country. The snow is too deep and soft, and there are no hills to ski on. The woods are so thick it is impossible to travel through them with a pair of skis. Even long snowshoes are a disadvantage in the woods, and most people use the little bear paws that can turn around on a dot. Most of the time I strapped on snowshoes and went out to watch the deer in their yard, behind the camp. There were seven deer in the yard, and I recognized the doe we had rescued from her icy bath in the St. John River.

When the snow is deep the deer live on cedar buds. They "yard"—collect in groups and trample down paths under a cedar grove, chewing off the boughs as high as they can reach. Their small, sharp hoofs and spindly legs wallow mercilessly in the deep snow.

In the old days when lumber camps used deer meat as a source of food, deer were cornered in the deep snow and slaughtered with an ax. I should imagine it was an inhuman exhibition, and I'm glad it was stopped. Deer grow a heavier coat of hair in the winter, and the bucks lose their antlers. They spend a great deal of their time bedded in the snow and sleeping, or munching on the cedar trees, walking slowly and awkwardly along their labyrinthine paths. They are timid animals and I had to use great stealth to be able to watch them from an advantageous position. I approached the yard where the wind was blowing toward me, being careful not to disturb any snow on branches or allow my snowshoes to make the least sound.

My hikes on snowshoes were slow because I always stopped to inspect the animal tracks along the trail. Rabbit paths were numerous, and the partridge tracks around the camp looked like a hen yard. We spread bread crumbs for the gorbies—"Whisky Jack," "Woodsman's Ghost" or "Canada Jay"—a dirty-gray, noisy bird that hangs around camps in the woods. Lumberjacks say they are the reincarnation of other departed lumberjacks. They are numerous and thieving, and wherever you are eating a lunch in the woods you will see a gorby perched on a tree limb, watching for a chance to steal a doughnut.

One of the most interesting of the woods birds is the pileated woodpecker, or "Cock of the Woods." They are rarely seen except in the deep woods, and even lumbering activities will drive them farther back. They are beautiful in flight when the clear black and white markings show under their wings. They are amazingly large birds with a high, red crest on their heads.

"Did you see an 'otter run' today?" Curly asked.

"An 'otter run'? I never heard of that. There are otter tracks on the beaver dam, if that's what you mean."

"No, I mean an 'otter run' on a high bank of an open brook where the otter slides down."

"What do they do that for?"

"Just playing, I guess. It gets icy and they slide easy."

I was suspicious. "I suppose they skid playfully on their bottoms and yip, or whatever an otter does to yip."

Curly was insulted. "No, they really do."

He may be right. I don't know. I'll have to see it before I believe it, but I do know that the otter is the most playful of all wild animals.

Chapter 37

Beaver Trappers

We had been the only residents at Nine Mile through most of the winter, but one day a Taylor Cub plane landed on the river above the rapids, and three trappers walked down to camp.

"Does the game warden live here?" they asked Curly.

"I'm the game warden. What can I do for you?"

"We'd like to trap beaver around here and since we aren't familiar with the country, we thought you might help us with this map."

"You plan to make your headquarters here?" Curly asked.

"That's what we thought."

"Can you play poker?" I butted in.

They brought in their supplies and equipment by plane and settled in the old lumber camp above us. Freddy, who later ferried bombers to England, was a short-statured Swede. Clyde Leach of Ashland was the information bureau, as he knew as much about the habits of beaver as the beavers did themselves. Scotty McCormack was the third of this industrious and adventure-loving trio.

We were delighted. They didn't come down to the camp often because they thought they were bothering us. After being there a while, they could easily understand how much bother they were. I had someone to eat the mass of food I cooked. I cut hair, washed union suits, made parkas, sewed buttons, darned socks and I liked it. It was company.

They later moved their "hangar" in front of our camp when the snow had drifted and packed over the uneven ice, and we could see them coming and going about their work. Beaver trapping with a plane is quick and efficient, and covers more territory in one day than the old trapper could in two weeks. Freddy was a north woods pilot. He knew the quick changes in weather, and he took no daredevil chances. With Clyde or Scotty he would cruise the beaver territory that was open to trapping, land on small lakes whenever a beaver house was sighted, and set the traps.

A beaver house is a rounded mound of packed small trees, twigs and earth, sometimes ten feet high, but averaging four feet. The base is set in water, in a bog or small pond that the beavers have flooded for protection by damming a brook or stream. There are two openings to the house, underwater, but the beavers sleep and eat on shelves in the hollowed interior of their house. They venture forth to hunt for food or to repair their dam.

A beaver is a brick mason without a union card. He is also an excellent engineer. Yet beavers are quite dumb animals in many ways. It is hard to drive them away by destroying their dams, as they persistently rebuild them. They are easily trapped, which is one of the reasons they were almost exterminated in the state of Maine. Due to wildlife conservation and strict laws protecting beavers, they are increasing, and in many places they are pests when they flood farmland and highways with their dams.

They cut poplars and other soft wood for food, gnawing the bark from the twigs and casting the wood out of the house at the opening where the current can carry it away. The wood they cut does not keep. It gets "sour," and the beaver explores his little lake, looking for fresh food. He stops at breathing holes that are kept open through the ice, and he repairs his dam.

"Bank" beaver, the lone beaver who digs his den in the bank of a river and cuts food as he needs it, is still a mystery. Whether he is a lazy beaver or one who has lost his mate is not known for a certainty.

After trappers locate houses, they can tell that they are occupied if the snow is soft and moist at the "smoke hole"—the top of the house where steam from the animal's body warmth escapes. Traps are set, frequently a deep-water set, known as a siwash. The trappers cut a hole through the ice, pound two stakes in on a slant and build a platform across the stakes. The trap is set on the platform and tied to the stake. Small pieces of poplar are nailed or tied above the trap. The beaver steps on the platform to get the poplar. The trap springs, falls from the platform, and the beaver is drowned.

It is unwise as well as illegal to trap near a beaver house, as only the little ones are caught. Farther away from the house, the prize is a big beaver, and sometimes a "blanket" beaver—a pelt that will stretch over seventy inches. This number is determined by adding the length and the width of a stretched pelt.

Beaver trapping is cold, hard work. The trapper walks long distances, carries a knapsack loaded with traps, chops holes through two and three feet of ice, and works in water with bare hands. Cyril Jandreau and Joe Giguare were trapping on Ross Lake one winter. They didn't have the advantage of an airplane, and they walked fifteen and twenty miles a day on snowshoes, eating lunches on the trail and working until late at night, fleshing beaver pelts.

Sometimes the skinning is done where the beaver is caught, as they are too heavy to carry. But with the plane, our trappers could bring them back to their headquarters, and the dogs had the carcasses for food. Curly sliced steaks from a hindquarter of a beaver and fried them. He said he liked them but I never could eat any. Many people like beaver tail. They sear it on hot coals, or dip it into a pail of boiling water to remove the outer skin, then slice it and fry it. They say it tastes like bone marrow, but I never could bring myself to eat that either.

We hadn't been lucky enough that fall to get horse meat for the dogs, and the beaver carcasses were manna from heaven. The dogs liked them. Poo-Poo could eat a small beaver at one sitting, and he often sneaked one out of the shed and hid it in his kennel. We could hear him gnawing his stolen feast at night.

"How do you suppose that dog got that meat?" Curly asked.

"He was loose a while this morning when you took them out."

"I'll have to take it away from him. He'll get so fat he won't be able to pull a pound."

I could tell the moment Curly took the meat away. Poo-Poo howled "Wa-oooo!"

The trappers worked hard and would be gone for three or four days at a time when they were trapping or cruising some small pond or brook that was accessible only on snowshoes. They caught over a hundred beavers that winter in the territory around our camp.

Evenings when they were home we visited them or they came down to our camp for supper and a game of poker or black-jack. If we called on them for supper, we played hearts, and the losers had to haul water, cook supper and wash dishes. When they had beavers to skin and stretch, we sat and watched them.

"Look at the funny claw on this beaver!" I exclaimed.

"Where?"

"On one of his front feet."

"Oh, that's his toothpick. They all have that."

"Toothpick? Sure, like an 'otter run,' I suppose."

"Well, look at it. Doesn't it look like a toothpick? They use it to pick the splinters out of their teeth."

Clyde was a genius at stretching a pelt on the wide boards, old doors and tabletops that they used for the purpose. He pulled and stretched evenly all around, holding with a small nail at every half inch and quarter inch, and paring off the great amount of fat that clings to the hide.

A stretched beaver pelt is almost white on the inside, and when it is dry, it is crackly and stiff, and oval in shape. The fur itself is a shaggy and ragged brown, but the long "guard" hairs are plucked or sheared from a beaver pelt before it is made into the beautiful furs for the market.

One morning Curly shot a mink near the pump, and it netted us twelve dollars. A mink is a small animal but the hide is tougher than muskrat and the fur is a silky, dark brown. Before a finished pelt is sent to a fur dealer, an interesting piece of work must be done. On some animals the skinning is done to the last detail of little ears and toenails. The slender bone in the tail is removed. I have skinned quite a few different types of fur-bearing animals—mink, muskrat, beaver, fox, bobcat and otter—and of all Maine furs, I think otter is the most beautiful. It is a silky, true black fur, and has the toughest hide of anything I have ever seen.

The trappers made the winter seem short for us. They brought in foodstuffs we ordered through them, mailed letters for us and traded store bread for the home-baked loaves I made. We liked the store bread better. Freddy brought in five gallons of ice cream that didn't last through the day. We buried it in a snowbank and spent our time running back and forth from camp to ice cream. Needless to say we didn't eat anything else that day. They brought in candy, oranges, lettuce, celery, tomatoes and ginger ale.

They flew to Lac Frontiere on Sunday, landed on the North West Branch of the St. John River, and flew passengers. Freddy was a hero. The people gathered from miles around for a ride in the "hairplane," and Lac Frontiere was crowded with these "tourists." The girls fell in love with Freddy and congregated at the hotel to greet him and sent him blushing furiously to the safety of his room.

I went to Portage by plane for a week's visit. When I came back a crestfallen husband confessed he had broken the meat grinder on Lac Frontiere "bully" beef, and had sprained his thumb. A week later, the trappers finished their work and moved out. We were alone again, in sole possession of everything we surveyed.

When it came time for Curly to make the rounds of the sugar camps, we knew that winter was almost gone and spring was definitely on its way. Sugaring is quite an industry along both sides of the boundary. When the pulp and pine were cut off the Province of Quebec, they were quickly replaced by maples and beeches, and almost every range-road family had a sugar house. Thousands of gallons of syrup were boiled down and stored in storehouses at Lac Frontiere and St. Pamphile. One storehouse in Lac Frontiere exploded, and for miles around, the trees and village were plastered with syrup. They still talk about it there, and call it the Brown Snowstorm.

Just to be sure that they weren't eating deer meat in the sugar houses on our side of the boundary, Curly visited each camp from Daaquam to St. Pamphile. He tasted and complimented the maple-sugar products, and came home with a loaded knapsack. He had little birch-bark cones of hardened sugar, gallon jugs of syrup, little molded sugar houses and cans of *la tire*—a thick, tasty syrup. He looked rather green around the gills, and when I suggested we have a light supper of flapjacks and the new syrup, he groaned.

"But don't you want a light supper?" I asked.

"Nope."

"What have you been doing, drinking sap from the pails?"

"Nope, but I tasted the syrup at Belanger's camp, then I tasted the syrup at Dubois's camp, and then I went to Pelchat's camp and tasted the syrup, and oh-h-h-h, I've got an awful bellyache!"

Chapter 38

Breaking Camp

Winters in the woods are long. Many weeks would go by during which we never saw another person or varied our daily schedule of three meals a day and ten hours of sleep. We measured time by incidents, and years by winters. One year might be the Cold Winter, another year the Big Snow Winter.

There is an enchantment about the wilderness, especially to those who have lived in civilization. At first you are acutely aware of the "wide open spaces feeling," and then you grow accustomed to it and feel possessive. The tall spruces and quiet shadows of the thick forests are a bit overwhelming until familiarity with them impresses you with the idea that the trees are but somber giants passively brooding through ages of time. Though the dark quietness of the woods is its most noticeable feature, you cannot miss the soft chattering, whirring and singing of the little forest animals. You cannot overlook the dappled sunshine flickering on cool, mossy carpets.

Living in the woods also means living near the water, either on lakes or rivers. The desire to live near the water is as old as mankind, and the woodsman in his primitive way of life strongly feels the seasonal moods of north woods lakes and rivers. When cold weather comes and the water rests quietly, the wilderness and its people wait with it for the gay freedom and exhilaration of spring. The activity through the summer months is a sharp contrast to the sleepy winters, and fall is spent in scurrying for food to store away before hibernation.

The fascination of the wilderness isn't very easily explained. It is something you have to like to enjoy. You have to take it as it is because it is too big to be changed within the short span of a lifetime.

I shall never forget the first time I was left alone. I walked through the camp merely to assure myself that there really wasn't anyone with me. The empty rooms were oppressive. I felt panicky and wanted to get outside where I wouldn't notice it so much. The immensity of the outdoors, the lonely wildness of the forests and the singing wind over the treetops only made me feel insignificant. I was but a tiny dot on this bit of wooded landscape. I waited. The air was chilly and when I went back to the warm fire in the kitchen stove, the camp was more like a protective shelter than a prison. After that I never minded staying alone. I stayed alone ten days at a time, with the nearest human being fifteen miles away. It didn't seem like ten days. I don't know that I accomplished a great deal during that time, yet I was busy. I do remember frying doughnuts at three o'clock one morning, probably just for something to do.

Time is of no consequence in the woods, but it has to be spent. I shoveled paths, filled up the wood boxes, played the radio, knitted stockings, sewed and worked on a patchwork quilt. Curly and I felt that our time was our own and we had a priceless freedom away from the restraining conventions of civilization.

The advent of spring brought with it the fact that only a few more months of Nine Mile life were to be ours. We had asked for a transfer, not because we wanted to leave but because we decided it would be best with a baby. I don't think I had realized before that Curly and I would be leaving before winter came again, and it startled me when I thought about how much we would miss the people we had lived with for so long. The sharing of the past winters had made us feel as though we were one big family, despite the many miles that lay between us. We took a few last trips on the river, and we visited the trout pool on Soper Brook for the May fishing.

On our last visit into Churchill, Mrs. Deblois brought out the cookies and cold milk that Curly and I always lunched on. It wasn't saying good-bye because there is no such thing as saying good-bye to the woods. You always come back to it. Mrs. Giguare stopped us when we went by her camp and presented me with a diaper bag for the expected addition to the family. Mrs. Giguare had eight children and had never been to a hospital when any of them were born. Joe Giguare was as good a midwife as there was in the country. We stopped at the post office at Clayton and had some of Miss Colson's pumpkin pie, and I wondered again how she kept her kitchen so shiny and clean.

Mrs. Bridges helped me clean the camp. I returned all the fire warden's dishes that I had borrowed. We sold what we could and donated the rest. The hardest part was selling the dogs and outfit, and a friend of ours offered to take them. We knew they would have a good home, but there was a lump in my throat when I saw Beer and Pretzel sitting dumbly on the back seat of the car that was to take them away, with Poo-Poo gleefully perched in front, elated at the prospects of riding for a change.

We couldn't part with Loupe. He was old and faithful and had worked hard. He deserved the best we could give him. Since we have left the country, we have kept track of our dogs, as we still call them. Poo-Poo is on a farm and heaven help the chickens! Beer and Pretzel were later bought by the timber cruiser who used them while working for the original buyer.

In July, I went to Milo where Penny was born. When Curly came down he brought news of his transfer. We were going to a new wilderness. Perhaps it wouldn't be spruce country; perhaps it would be pine. There would be more roads and more civilization, but we wouldn't be far from woods and water. Curly could forget the few French words he knew, and my new Quebec accent could get rusty. One thing was sure—it would be a new adventure.

Afterword

A lot has changed since a twenty-year-old Helen Leidy drove 400 miles from her Fort Kent home and into the wilderness to teach school at Churchill Depot. And a lot has not.

The great wilderness is still there, perhaps even more so, despite advances in technology, equipment and general comforts. This region remains the largest wilderness in the continental United States—vast acres of unorganized territories, lakes, streams, mountains and forest.

Logging and other businesses in the woods-based industry remain important to the Maine economy, particularly in northern and eastern Maine, but the type of logging operations described by Helen Hamlin is long gone—the legendary river-driver has been replaced by canoeists and the bateaus by canoes.

In no particular order, here is what has become of some of the key players in Helen Hamlin's *Nine Mile Bridge*.

Churchill Depot

When Churchill Depot was a thriving community during the late 1920s and 1930s, there were more than twenty buildings, including houses, sheds, workshops, a boardinghouse, a storehouse, and a school. Helen Hamlin actually witnessed the last gasps of

The remains of the dam at Churchill Depot, 1961. This dam was breeched in the 1950s and has been replaced twice.

this village—it was essentially shuttered in 1938, the same year she finished her year of teaching.

By the late 1960s, only seven of the original buildings remained. Today, the boardinghouse and storehouse stand alone as reminders of that once-bustling settlement.

The old boardinghouse has fallen into disrepair, although it was shored up in 1996 by a group of volunteers that recognized its historic significance. There have been discussions, driven by the Allagash Alliance, about restoring the building to create an historic museum of the North Woods and Allagash region, but no official plans have been implemented.

Since acquiring the Churchill Depot site in the 1960s as part of the Allagash Wilderness Waterway, the state of Maine has rebuilt Churchill Dam twice. It has also built a park manager's residence, a ranger cabin and a maintenance building, along with other facilities for waterway users, including a parking area, campsite and canoe landing.

The dam of Hamlin's era (built in 1925 by Great Northern Paper Company) was breached in 1958. A new timber-crib dam was built in 1968 about 300 feet upstream from the original dam. The 1968 dam also deteriorated and was replaced by a concrete structure in 1997.

Umsaskis Lake

Umsaskis Lake is an important part of the Allagash Wilderness Waterway. There is a ranger's cabin and a warden's cabin on the lake. However, the cabin that Helen and Curly lived in has long been torn down, as have the sporting camps mentioned by Helen Hamlin.

Nine Mile Bridge

In 1927, Edward "King" La Croix built a road into Nine Mile so he could get supplies to his backwoods operations. In 1931, he placed a bridge—which was a discarded one-lane bridge from St. George, Quebec, that he had brought into Maine in pieces—across the St. John River at Nine Mile. The bridge, which gave Helen's book its name, remained in place for many years, but was finally destroyed by ice and washed away.

The Hamlins' cabin at Nine Mile Bridge is also long gone.

Allagash River

The Allagash River was the target of serious preservation efforts starting in the 1960s. The result of that effort was the creation of the Allagash Wilderness Waterway—a region that encompasses both Churchill Depot and Umsaskis Lake—which was established by the Maine Legislature in 1966 to preserve,

Photo courtesy of Dean B. Bennett

The boardinghouse where Helen Hamlin lived at Churchill Depot, 1998.

protect and enhance the area. The Waterway is a 92-mile-long ribbon of lakes, ponds, rivers and streams that winds through the vast Maine wilderness. Protection was further enhanced in 1970 when it became the first state-managed river in the National Wild and Scenic Rivers System. The Waterway is very popular for canoe trips (private outdoor companies provide guided trips) and with sportsmen and -women.

St. John River

The old Nine Mile Bridge was on the St. John River, a river roughly 420 miles long that forms part of Maine's northern border with Canada. Like the Allagash, the St. John is popular with canoeists and sportsmen and -women. Many of the old landings and logging depots have been reclaimed by the wilderness. One stretch of the river flows for 130 miles without passing a single settlement.

Lumber and Logging

The great logging operations and the traditional logging camps discussed by Helen Hamlin are mostly part of history. Most symbolically, the legendary log drives and rivermen that embodied this way of life—and contributed to its rugged mythology—are long gone. The last drive came down a Maine river in the 1970s.

Still, there are reminders deep in the wilderness that highlight the ambition, drive, ingenuity and sheer hard work that characterized the lumber and logging industry of the late 1800s and early 1900s.

Remnants of the original cable Tramway—built in the early 1900s to carry logs overland from Eagle Lake to Chamberlain Lake—are still visible. The Tramway was essentially a small railroad pulled by a cable loop six thousand feet long, which replaced an older and less-efficient lock-dam system of moving logs. Steel trucks attached to the cable carried the logs across three thousand feet from the northern end of Chamberlain Lake.

Photo courtesy of Dean B. Bennett

The site where the old Nine Mile Bridge spanned the St. John River.

Photo courtesy of Dean B. Bennett

An aerial view of Churchill Depot in 2002, with Churchill Lake visible in the distance.

The schoolhouse where Helen Hamlin taught at Churchill Depot.
This photo was reproduced from an unknown newspaper.

Since the Tramway was a loop, each car would drop its logs into
the lake, then loop back for another load. At peak production, a
half-million board feet of logs could be transported in a single day.

Even more dramatic was the old Eagle Lake and West
Branch Railroad, which replaced the Tramway in 1926 to carry
logs from Eagle and Churchill lakes to Umbazookus Lake. This
railroad made it easier to move logs to the famed Penobscot
River via its West Branch. This railroad was a stunning techno-
logical achievement, driven by La Croix. The railroad ran thirteen miles through the heart of the wilderness and featured a
90-ton steam locomotive that was converted to oil, a 1,500-foot-
long railroad trestle across Chamberlain Lake, large conveyor
belts, and required that oil be shipped in via scow to keep the
trains running. In an average week, 6,500 cords of wood moved
across the track.

Today, the rusted hulks of two massive locomotives can still be found at Tramway between Eagle Lake and Churchill Lake. Volunteers have righted the locomotives and cleared some of the old rail line to make a walking path.

Finally, there will likely never be a Helen and Curly Hamlin again either. Not only has technology reduced the sheer isolation for those living even in the remote Maine wilderness, but fish and game wardens no longer spend entire winters in remote cabins. It was a difficult job in what some might call a romantic time.

And luckily, Helen Hamlin has preserved that time for eternity.